UNDERSTANDING THE EURO

The Clear and Concise Guide to the New Trans-European Economy

CHRISTIAN N. CHABOT

McGraw-Hill
New York   San Francisco   Washington, D.C.   Auckland   Bogotá
Caracas   Lisbon   London   Madrid   Mexico City   Milan
Montreal   New Delhi   San Juan   Singapore
Sydney   Tokyo   Toronto

Library of Congress Cataloging-in-Publication Data

Chabot, Christian N.
    Understanding the euro : the clear and concise guide to the new
trans-european economy / by Christian N. Chabot.
      p. cm.
    Includes index.
    ISBN 0-07-134388-1
    1. Euro. 2. Money—European Union countries. 3. Monetary policy—
European Union countries. 4. Monetary unions—European Union
countries. 5. European Union countries—Economic integration.
I. Title.
HG925.C46   1999
332.4'94—dc21   98-49945
                                                                         CIP

McGraw-Hill

A Division of The **McGraw·Hill** Companies

1 2 3 4 5 6 7 8 9 0 DOC/DOC 9 0 3 2 1 0 9 8

ISBN 0-07-134388-1

*The editing supervisor was Christine Furry and the production supervisor was Tina Cameron.
It was set in Times Roman by North Market Street Graphics.*

Printed and bound by R. R. Donnelley & Sons Company.

McGraw-Hill books are available at special quantity discounts to use as premiums and sales
promotions, or for use in corporate training programs. For more information, please write to
the Director of Special Sales, McGraw-Hill, 11 West 19th Street, New York, NY 10011. Or
contact your local bookstore.

For Angela

C O N T E N T S

Chapter 5

ACKNOWLEDGMENTS

Special thanks go to the Robert Bosch Foundation in Stuttgart, Germany, whose funding enabled an extended stay in the EMU and Economics divisions of the Deutsche Bundesbank during the euro's most exciting hour. Fellowship particulars were organized by Dr. Peter Theiner, Jacqueline Von Saldern, and Dirk Reichel at the Foundation, and also by Dr. Reiner König, Dr. Heinz Herrmann, and Klaus Weber at the Bundesbank. The unrestricted interview access to key Bundesbank, EMI, and Bank of England officials afforded by the fellowship made this book a reality. I owe a particular debt of gratitude to Bundesbank economist Dr. Bettina Landau, who not only made a return visit possible, but also provided invaluable insights during my time there. Thanks go to Petra Arzbach and her assistants at the Bundesbank library.

The manuscript itself received critical input from a variety of specialists, including Malin Haugwitz and Dr. Werner Becker at Deutsche Bank and Sven Peterson and Helmut Wacket at the Bundesbank. Clark Parsons, Mark Walker, Jill Clark, and Sudha David provided guidance in a range of areas. The journalistic expertise of Gregg and Dan Chabot also weigh heavily on this edition. Any errors or omissions, however, are mine alone.

Support from Greg and Kay Harmeyer, Brett Chabot, and Mary Ellen Chabot was absolutely indispensable. Thanks go to Rob Reid, who believed in the project from the outset and introduced me to our mutual agent, Alice Martell. I appreciate Alice's consummate professionalism, as well as her unfailing encouragement and advice. Thanks also go to Mary Glenn, my editor at McGraw-Hill.

Finally, I owe the greatest debt of gratitude to my wife, Angela, for her unqualified support and advice from the very beginning.

INTRODUCTION

The euro is here.

Since January 1, 1999, the world has witnessed one of the most profound and far-reaching economic events of modern history. On that date, the European Union (EU) launched the final stage of Economic and Monetary Union (EMU), thereby creating a new trans-European currency, the *euro,* that will back well over $6000 billion of new goods and services in its first year. This monetary revolution creates the second largest economic bloc in the world, a single market of almost 300 million people, a drastically changed European business environment, and the first potential challenge to the supremacy of the U.S. dollar. Hence, the euro affects not only the bankers, financiers, and economists of Europe, but also executives, managers, investors, marketers, analysts, attorneys, journalists, and politicians worldwide.

The euro's effects are so permanent and far-reaching that people unfamiliar with the currency's basic evolution, structure, and meaning now find themselves with a massive professional blind spot. Of course, public discussion about EMU has had a dreamlike quality ever since its inception in 1992, with most observers assuming it would never happen. Petty political disputes and euro-skepticism dominated news on the subject for years, while the engine of technical preparation hummed quietly in the background. But the last remnants of doubt have disintegrated. The euro is now the official currency of Austria, Belgium, Finland, France, Germany, Ireland, Italy, Luxembourg, the Netherlands, Portugal, and Spain.

On one extreme, the introduction of the euro has been called "an opportunity to achieve the biggest welfare and efficiency gains of any economic event or system in postwar European history" and "a watershed for European business." From this perspective the euro will unify western Europe, encourage competition, revolutionize finance, and usher Europe into its greatest economic era. On the other extreme, monetary union has been called a "leap in the dark," "a blind stab at the future," "a flawed scheme," and even "economic and political castration." The breadth of opinion on the subject is hardly surprising, as nearly every aspect of the euro involves complicated problems and financial relationships. In fact, it is difficult to read even the most introductory news on the subject without getting lost in a sea of jargon, bias, and confusion. Readers are often left with the following questions:

> What exactly is the euro and why was it created?
>
> When, where, and how is the euro being introduced?
>
> How does the euro change European monetary policy?
>
> How does the euro affect international business environments?
>
> What specific effects does the euro have on industries, firms, and investments worldwide?

The goal of this book is to answer these questions and many others in simple, unbiased, and straightforward terms. It answers the most pressing questions about the euro and serves as an accurate and up-to-date guide to the new currency's worldwide ramifications.

To ensure that these issues are handled clearly and logically, the book is written in a consistent question-and-answer format. Each chapter offers a series of detailed but "plain English" answers to the most critical questions about the euro and the meaning of EMU. It is designed to be read cover to cover, as each question builds on a general framework for understanding the issues involved in the introduction of the euro. But it needn't be read strictly sequentially. The index and glossary provide easy access to specific questions in all areas, so that the book functions as a convenient reference guide long after its first reading.

Topics are divided thematically into five chapters. Chapter 1, "Introduction to the Euro," offers a general orientation for those readers who are totally new to the subject. Chapter 2, "Birth of the Euro," then presents crucial contextual information and describes the basic economic and financial features of monetary union. Chapter 3, "Monetary Policy in the Euro Zone," outlines the new structure of monetary policy in Europe, with particular emphasis on the structure and operation of the newly created European Central Bank (ECB). Chapter 4, "The Euro's Effects on Business Environments Worldwide," then turns to the euro's immediate and long-term effects on business environments and capital markets worldwide. Chapter 5, "The Euro's Effects on Firms and Individuals Worldwide," concludes by explaining the specific consequences that the new trans-European currency has for industries, firms, and investments.

A B B R E V I A T I O N S

EC	European Community
ECB	European Central Bank
ECOFIN	EU Council of economics and finance ministers
ECSC	European Coal and Steel Community
Ecu	European Currency Unit
EEC	European Economic Community
EMI	European Monetary Institute
EMS	European Monetary System
EMU	Economic and Monetary Union
ERM	Exchange Rate Mechanism
ESCB	European System of Central Banks
EU	European Union
Euratom	European Atomic Energy Community
Euribor	European-Inter-Bank Offer Rate
FASB	Federal Accounting Standards Bureau
GDP	Gross Domestic Product
IPO	Initial Public Offering
Libor	London Interbank Offered Rate
REIT	Real Estate Investment Trust
SEC	U.S. Securities and Exchange Commission

CHAPTER

Introduction to the Euro

The monetary revolution embodied in the euro involves far more than the elimination of 11 national currencies and the distribution of colorful new banknotes and coins across Europe. It entails the solidification of the European Union's common market for goods and services, major structural changes in countries plagued by fiscal imprudence, and the reorganization of monetary policy in some of the world's most advanced industrialized economies. Though at first glance it may seem that a new trans-European currency would hold little significance outside of banking and tourist circles, the euro has in fact invaded nearly every sector of the world economy, defining the terms of major elections and policy debates and rattling the international business environment.*

Yet for all of the attention, the euro is a deeply misunderstood creature. Especially among non-Europeans, who had little reason to think about the euro before its arrival, the new currency still seems like the unreal fantasy of a handful of distant countries. This unfamiliarity stems not only from the remoteness of European life, but also from the fact that EU governments have made almost no effort to explain the euro and its meaning to non-Europeans, even though millions of dollars of internal EU education campaigns have left even the average European feeling less than well informed about the euro.[1] Hence, before we delve into some of the more complicated aspects of monetary union, it is appropriate to introduce the "euro basics."

1. What is the euro?

The euro is the newly created currency of the European Union, a currency that became legal tender on January 1, 1999. By

---

* For convenience, "Europe" in this book refers to the 15 members of the European Union. This is in no way intended to understate the critical importance of eastern Europe to continental affairs.

FIGURE 1-1

Euroland and the European Union.

Members of the European Union: Austria, Belgium, Denmark, Finland, France, Germany, Great Britain, Greece, Ireland, Italy, Luxembourg, the Netherlands, Portugal, Spain, and Sweden.

Members of the Single-Currency Area: Austria, Belgium, Finland, France, Germany, Ireland, Italy, Luxembourg, the Netherlands, Portugal, and Spain.

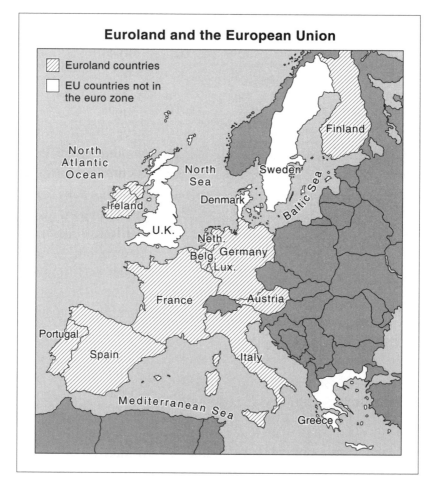

2002, freshly printed euro notes and coins will replace the Austrian schilling, Belgian franc, Finnish markka, French franc, German mark, Irish punt, Italian lira, Luxembourg franc, Dutch guilder, Portuguese escudo, and Spanish peseta as the exclusive legal tender of those 11 nations. These countries, collectively referred to as Euroland, now share a common money, a single monetary policy, and a single foreign exchange rate policy. Old national currencies are being permanently eliminated.

Typically underestimated, currencies play a crucial role in the functioning of modern economies. They not only serve as a *standardized value of measurement,* so that we have a consistent way of expressing value, but they also function as an efficient *means of payment,* so that we don't have to list the price of every product in terms of the millionfold other products for which it could be traded. Equally important, currencies serve as a *store of value,* allowing us to transport wealth easily over a distance and to store it for indefinite periods of time. As Figure 1-1 shows, the euro now serves these crucial functions for the largest single-currency zone ever created, an area that stretches from the craggy coast of western Ireland to the hills of southern Sicily.

2. When is the euro coming?

The euro did not arrive overnight. As shown in Figure 1-2, it is being introduced in three distinct phases. Phase A began on May 2, 1998, and ended on January 1, 1999. It started with a special European Union summit in Brussels, a meeting whose central purpose was to determine which of the EU's 15 member nations would take part in monetary union. Before the Brussels summit, the choice of euro participants was one of the most controversial political issues in Europe, dominating nearly every discussion of economic and monetary union. Once the European Council finally announced the qualifying participants, however, the remaining eight months of Phase A witnessed (1) the establishment of a new European Central Bank (Europe's equivalent of the U.S. Federal Reserve), (2) final adjustments to national legal systems to accommodate a new currency, and (3) the first printing of euro notes and coins.

Phase B commenced on January 1, 1999. It began with the introduction of the euro as legal tender in the 11 countries that comprise the single-currency area. During Phase B, however, the euro exists only as a *book unit of account;* that is, no actual euro notes and coins are distributed. This means that the euro is currently employed in everything from personal checks, bank statements, electronic records, and accounting systems to multimillion-dollar corporate invoices and financial statements. The euro will not, however, actually enter the wallets of European citizens until Phase C.

Furthermore, the EU has adopted a "no compulsion, no prohibition" rule for the use of the euro during Phase B. In short, this means that those wanting to employ the euro as a book unit of account (e.g., in their bank accounts) in this period have the legal right to do so, but that no one can be forced. Hence, large multinational companies such as France's Alcatel, Germany's Daimler-Benz, Finland's Nokia, and the U.S.'s Chase Manhattan adopted the euro for European accounting and financial reporting purposes immediately on January 1, 1999, though they can't force any of their customers to pay in euro. Other businesses, including many small firms, will make the transition much later in Phase B. Of course, the economic magnitude of this "book currency" phase should not be underestimated, since cash-in-hand transactions comprise only a very small portion of all economic activity. In fact, partially for this reason, the total value of European banknotes in circula-

FIGURE 1-2

Introducing the euro in three phases.

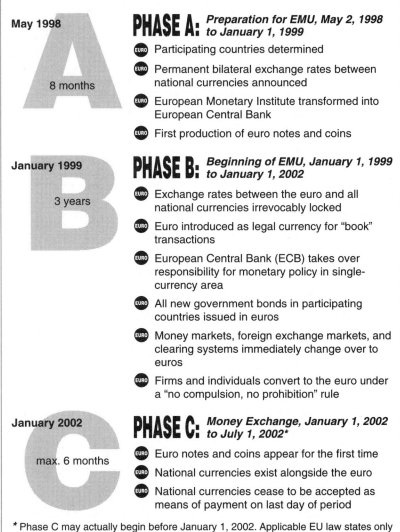

May 1998

8 months

PHASE A: *Preparation for EMU, May 2, 1998 to January 1, 1999*

- (EURO) Participating countries determined
- (EURO) Permanent bilateral exchange rates between national currencies announced
- (EURO) European Monetary Institute transformed into European Central Bank
- (EURO) First production of euro notes and coins

January 1999

3 years

PHASE B: *Beginning of EMU, January 1, 1999 to January 1, 2002*

- (EURO) Exchange rates between the euro and all national currencies irrevocably locked
- (EURO) Euro introduced as legal currency for "book" transactions
- (EURO) European Central Bank (ECB) takes over responsibility for monetary policy in single-currency area
- (EURO) All new government bonds in participating countries issued in euros
- (EURO) Money markets, foreign exchange markets, and clearing systems immediately change over to euros
- (EURO) Firms and individuals convert to the euro under a "no compulsion, no prohibition" rule

January 2002

max. 6 months

PHASE C: *Money Exchange, January 1, 2002 to July 1, 2002**

- (EURO) Euro notes and coins appear for the first time
- (EURO) National currencies exist alongside the euro
- (EURO) National currencies cease to be accepted as means of payment on last day of period

* Phase C may actually begin before January 1, 2002. Applicable EU law states only that this is the *latest* permissible starting date of the final phase. Phase C may also last less than six months.

tion has traditionally amounted to less than 6 percent of gross domestic product.[2]

Phase B lasts a maximum of three years and involves several major events. First, on January 1, 1999, European finance ministers irrevocably locked exchange rates between the euro and its 11 constituent currencies. Although the *bilateral* exchange rates had already been fixed in May of 1998 (e.g., how many Italian lira a French franc could buy), it wasn't until 1999 that *euro* exchange rates were determined (e.g., how many euro a French franc could buy). These rates, calculated by comparing the trading values of EMU currencies against the U.S. dollar on the last trading day of 1998, became permanent thereafter.

Phase B also entails the transfer of monetary policy authority to the European Central Bank (ECB). The ECB's predecessor, the European Monetary Institute (EMI), was founded in 1994 and worked for six years under the leadership of Alexandre Lamfalussy and Wim Duisenburg to establish the guidelines within which monetary policy would be conducted when the euro arrived. On June 1, 1998, however, the EMI became an obsolete institution and gave way to the European Central Bank, the EU's version of the U.S. Federal Reserve (see question 16). Subsequently, on January 1, 1999, the 11 national central banks of the single-currency zone became subordinate to the ECB.

Phase C will see the first introduction of euro banknotes and coins. It will be the only phase in which old national currencies actually exist alongside the euro. Consumers will be allowed to make cash transactions with national currencies *or* euros, although the European Central Bank will gradually take the old currencies out of circulation during this period. At the end of Phase C, the euro becomes the exclusive legal tender of the single-currency zone. National notes and coins will be exchanged for euros at banks for many years after the end of Phase C, but the euro alone will be accepted as *payment* after that phase.

European Union regulations state that Phase C must begin by January 1, 2002, and end by July 1, 2002, but it may begin earlier and end sooner. The European Council will probably decide when Phase C actually begins sometime before 2001. Individual governments will then decide for themselves how long the phase, once it begins simultaneously in all participating nations, will last in their own countries. France, for instance, has already announced that it will limit the length of Phase C to a maximum of six weeks because of the tremendous cost and confusion of doing business in multiple currencies (e.g., cash register transactions). Other countries are considering a "big bang" approach, in which the entire Phase C transition occurs over a week, or even a weekend.

No matter what the self-selected timing of individual nations, however, the introduction of the euro will be completed no later than by July 1, 2002.

3. What do euro notes and coins look like?

Though they usually serve more practical functions, currencies are an important source of national identity and symbolism. Typically adorned with the faces of national icons, including politicians, artists, writers, and scientists, they convey a sense of pride and prestige. Consider the German mark, a currency decorated with national heroes like Carl Friedrich Gauss and Clara Schumann and adored by the German public for its role in reestablishing economic normalcy after World War II and again during German reunification. Or pound sterling, which has borne the face of English royalty in the British Commonwealth for hundreds of years. Or the French franc, which features the portraits of Gustave Eiffel, Marie Curie, and Paul Cézanne.

Aware that the appearance of Europe's single currency would play a role in establishing public confidence in both the political and economic idea of a unified Europe, the European Monetary Institute held an official design competition between February and September of 1996. In addition to a few practical restrictions, competitors were prohibited from entering images that could be associated with any particular country, for fear of evoking bitter infighting and national rivalry. Images such as the Eiffel Tower, the leaning tower of Pisa, Beethoven, Bach, or Caravaggio were forbidden.

The contest winner was an Austrian designer named Robert Kalina, an employee of the Austrian National Bank. Kalina's design survived a survey of nearly 2000 taxi drivers, bank cashiers, and retailers as well as an official review panel composed of artists, marketers, and monetary specialists. Figure 1-3 shows the winning designs.

Consistent with competition requirements, each of the seven banknotes reflects a specific period of European history: Classical, Romanesque, Gothic, Renaissance, Baroque, the age of iron and glass, and Modern. As a theme, Kalina chose "bridges, gates, and windows," but none of his images is modeled after a particular European monument. Rather, they represent features that can be found in many parts of Europe. The face of each bill depicts a characteristic window or gateway from one of the historical periods set against the 12 stars of the European Union.* The back side of each portrays a picturesque but fictional bridge alongside a map of Europe. In the next few

---

* Why 12 stars? The official explanation is, "Against the background of blue sky, twelve golden stars form a circle, representing the union of the peoples of Europe. The number of stars is invariable, twelve being the symbol of perfection and entirety."

FIGURE 1-3

Euro notes and coins.

Notes: 5, 10, 20, 50, 100, 200, 500 euros. Draft banknote design
© European Monetary Institute, 1997; European Central Bank, 1998.

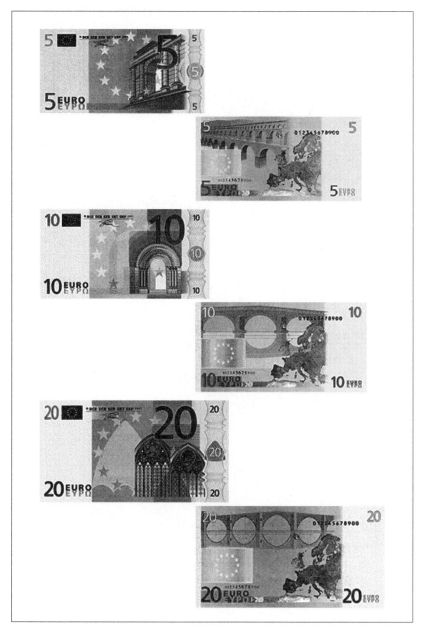

FIGURE 1-3

Euro notes and coins. (*Continued*)

Notes: 5, 10, 20, 50, 100, 200, 500 euros. Draft banknote design
© European Monetary Institute, 1997; European Central Bank, 1998.

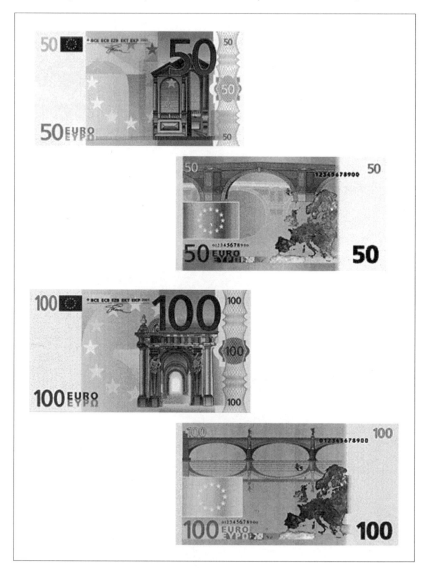

FIGURE 1-3

Euro notes and coins. (*Continued*)

Notes: 5, 10, 20, 50, 100, 200, 500 euros. Draft banknote design
© European Monetary Institute, 1997; European Central Bank, 1998.

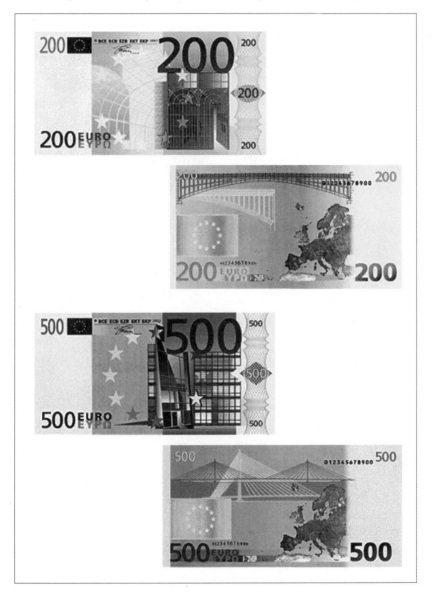

FIGURE 1-3

Euro notes and coins. (*Continued*)

Coins: 1, 2, 5, 10, 20, and 50 cents; 1, 2 euros. © German Federal Finance Ministry.

Note: The "reverse side" designs shown are those minted in the Federal Republic of Germany.

years, as many as 12 billion of these notes will be printed by 11 national presses.[3]

Euro coins were not part of the design competition. The faces of euro coins depict maps of Europe and the 12 stars of the European Union, while the reverse sides feature national symbols. Because euro coins are minted by the 11 individual countries (as opposed to the European Central Bank), each national government is responsible for the reverse side of those coins printed in its country. Since there are eight euro coins and 11 participating countries, there are now 88 such designs. Coin designs in Germany, for instance, include the Brandenburg Gate and the symbolic German eagle. Italian designs, selected in part by a national telephone poll, depict Leonardo da Vinci's *Renaissance Man* and Alessandro Botticelli's *Birth of Venus*. Between 1999 and 2002, nine national mints will produce over 76 billion euro coins.[4] All coins, regardless of country of origin, are accepted as payment in the entire single-currency zone.

The euro is associated with two other symbols as well. Just as dollar and yen denominations are symbolized by "$" and "¥," respectively, the euro is formally denoted with the newly designed "€" character. Also, the official International Standards Organization (ISO) code for euro is "EUR."

4. How does the European common market compare to the rest of the world?

The euro gives birth to one of the largest and most powerful trading blocs in the world, though only 11 of the EU's 15 member countries are currently participating. Although the introduction of the euro doesn't alter the fact that Euroland is composed of diverse and highly independent countries, it unquestionably strengthens the economic and political ties of the region and its accompanying "weight" in the world economy. Because the success of the euro will ultimately be determined by the collaboration of EU governments in a wide variety of areas, from the formulation of exchange rate policy to the harmonization of legal systems and security policy, the concept of western Europe as a single economic and political bloc is now more apt than ever.

Seen in this light, the euro significantly shifts the global balance of power. The new currency creates the second-largest single-currency area in the world, one that trails only the United States in total output. Euroland as a whole is responsible for nearly a fifth of global production, only slightly less than that attributable to the United States. When and if Great Britain, Sweden, Denmark, and Greece join the euro area, Europe will easily surpass the United States in total economic output. Already, Europe is home to more people (consumers, investors, and taxpayers) united by a single currency than is the United States or Japan.

Figure 1-4 provides a general comparison of the European Union (15 countries) and Euroland (11 countries) to the United States and Japan. (Figure 1-4*a* gives the same information shown visually in the bar graphs of Figure 1-4*b*. We'll use this format often throughout the book for clarity.)

Euroland, from the perspective of world trade and global finance, has become an economic superpower. Figure 1-5

FIGURE 1-4a

Just how big is Euroland?

	European Union	Euroland	USA	Japan
Population (millions)	374	290	268	126
Geographic area (sq. miles)	1,300,000	910,000	3,720,000	150,000
Gross Domestic Product ($billion)	8,093	6,309	7,819	4,223
GDP per person ($)	21,600	21,700	29,200	33,500

Sources: OECD, EU Commission, Deutsche Bank, IIE.

FIGURE 1-4b

Just how big is Euroland? (*Continued*)

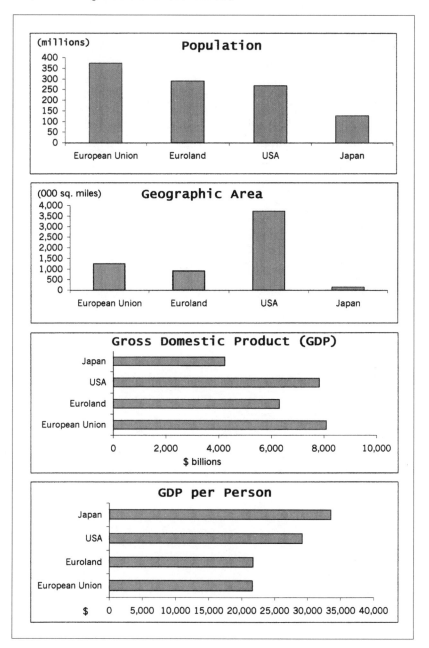

17

shows that Euroland is responsible for a tremendous proportion of world trade, exporting almost $1500 billion in 1997 and importing $1400 billion. (Figure 1-5a gives the same information shown in the bar graphs of Figure 1-5b.) Historically, Euroland and the United States have each contributed about the same amount to world trade, a figure that currently stands at about one-fifth. This implies that each region is home to a significant number of the large multinational corporations that are the powerhouses of international business. Indeed, of the world's 100 largest firms, 36 are European and 24 are American.[5]

European capital markets, however, pale in comparison to their immense, highly liquid American counterparts. Specifically, the American market for domestic securities is about twice as large as all Euroland markets combined. This leaves Euroland with combined equity and bond markets not much

FIGURE 1-5a

Euroland in the world economy.

	Euroland	United States	Japan
Exports ($ billion)	1,490	660	280
Imports ($ billion)	1,360	780	320
Share of world trade (%)	18.6	18.3	10.3
Share of world GDP (%)	19	20	8
Stock market capitalization ($ billion)	2,712	10,879	2,063
Bond market ($ billion)	4,700	10,200	4,100

Sources: Eurostat, World Bank, WTO, Deutsche Bundesbank, Federation of European Stock Exchanges, New York and Tokyo Stock Exchanges, IIE, *Die Woche*.

FIGURE 1-5b

Euroland in the world economy. (*Continued*)

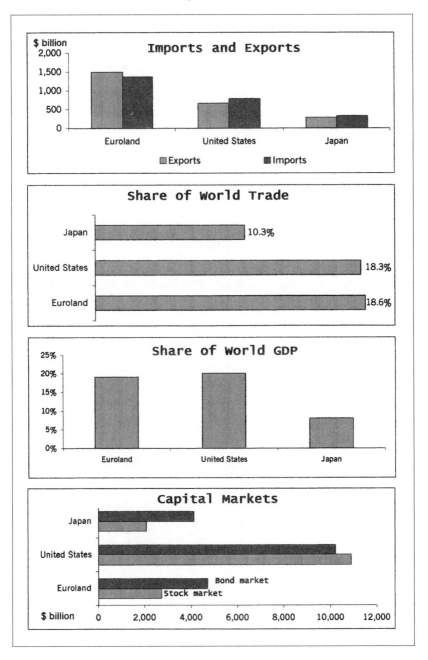

larger than Japan's, though some experts contend that the mere creation of a single currency removes barriers that have kept the European capital markets unnaturally constrained (see question 29). Only time will tell if such arguments are correct.

5. What requirements do countries have to fulfill in order to qualify for the euro?

Not just any country can adopt the euro. When EU leaders met in Maastricht, the Netherlands, in 1991 to draft the Treaty on European Union ("Maastricht Treaty"), they created specific economic hurdles, or entrance requirements, to be surmounted by any country wishing to participate.

Foremost, a country must be a member of the European Union. Membership in the EU requires, among other things, the removal of trade barriers and tariffs, the streamlining of customs, the elimination of passport controls, and the willing-ness to surrender limited political authority to an independent body. Such requirements are essential to the success of a common currency.

But EU countries themselves also have to clear significant economic hurdles. These five hurdles are known as the "convergence criteria," or the "Maastricht criteria."

The first is based on *price stability.* Specifically, countries must have a rate of consumer price inflation no more than 1.5 percent above that of the three countries in the EU with the lowest such inflation. When the European Council chose the first-round euro participants in May of 1998, this hurdle inflation rate was calculated to be 2.7 percent.

The second criterion concerns *government budget deficits.* In order to qualify for the euro, countries must have a ratio of general government borrowing to Gross Domestic Product (GDP) no greater than 3.0 percent, unless this ratio has declined substantially and continually and comes close to 3.0 percent.

The third requirement relates to *total government debt.* Countries must have a ratio of gross government debt to GDP no greater than 60 percent, unless this ratio is substantially and continually decreasing and is approaching 60 percent.

The fourth concerns *interest rates.* Euro hopefuls must have a nominal interest rate on long-term government bonds no more than 2 percent above that of the three EU members with the lowest such rate. When the first-round euro participants were announced in May of 1998, this rate was 7.8 percent.

The fifth criterion pertains to *exchange rate stability.* Countries must be members of the European Monetary System (see question 8) and their currencies must trade within the normal margins of fluctuation of that system. Put simply, potential participants must have stable currencies.

The EU created the five convergence criteria to ensure that (1) any country joining monetary union is fiscally responsible, and (2) participating countries are sufficiently similar (or "convergent") to warrant a single monetary policy. The inclusion of a country with high inflation, volatile exchange rates, skyrocketing interest rates, or a huge budget deficit would alert financial markets that the euro is a risky and unstable project, primarily because the inclusion would pose a grave threat to developing a single set of interest rates for the area as a whole (see question 13). Because the euro's standing in financial markets will shape the tone and pace of European economic growth for the next century, many EU leaders feel that the convergence criteria are a fair price of admission to the single-currency zone.

Ironically, for a long time after 1992 it looked as though very few EU countries would qualify for the euro. As the current president of the European Central Bank pointed out after examining the key statistics for 1995, "the average fiscal deficit in the European Union came out at 4.7 percent of GDP, while public debt has been going up almost without interruption since the early 1970s, to almost 70 percent of GDP. As things stand now, not all member states will be in on . . . EMU."[6] The convergence criteria posed substantial hurdles for Euroland governments. In fact, even the United States, with an average annual budget deficit of over 4 percent, would not have qualified for the euro between 1990 and 1994.

Yet the European Union was determined to have its single currency. In what was perhaps the most impressive round of fiscal budget tightening and creative accounting the world has ever seen, nation after nation implemented the reforms necessary to make the euro a reality. Italy created a 12-trillion-lira "euro tax" to shape up its government budget deficit. Germany sold several million tons of strategic oil reserves. France changed the accounting rules on 37.5 billion francs sitting in France Telecom's pension fund, effectively moving the savings into government coffers. It then hiked corporate tax rates for the nation's largest firms and even applied it retroactively to profits made in the previous year. Sweden made deep cuts to its welfare state, sparking political turmoil. Finland slashed its central government budget by over 45 billion markka between 1991 and 1996. Ultimately, the years of reform succeeded. On May 2, 1998, the European Council decided that 11 of the 12 EU countries wanting to adopt the euro fulfilled the five "convergence criteria."

But fulfilling the convergence criteria is not a one-time event. Because the euro's architects knew that fiscal responsibility would be meaningful only if maintained, the EU drafted the "Stability & Growth Pact" at the 1996 Dublin Summit. Designed to enforce long-term fiscal discipline, the main feature of the pact is an agreement to fine Euroland countries that run "excessive deficits." If a country runs a budget deficit that exceeds 3.0 percent of GDP, it must pay non-interest-bearing deposits to the European Union equivalent to 0.2 percent of its GDP, plus 0.1 percent of GDP for every percentage point of deficit beyond 3.0 percent (up to a maximum of 0.5 percent of GDP). This is a massive amount of money, currently ranging from about $60 million in Luxembourg to $7 billion in Germany. If the troubled country is unable to alleviate its excessive budget deficit within two years, the European Commission considers the deposit a *fine* and distributes it among other members of the euro zone. Exceptions may be granted if the troubled country is in recession.* Because the pact sets strict limits on government deficits and fiscal imprudence in the EU, it is considered one of the most important features of monetary union.

6. Why are some European countries not participating in monetary union?

Not a single eastern European country, from Albania and Slovenia to the Baltic States, is a part of Economic and Monetary Union. These countries are simply not members of the European Union, and therefore not entitled to membership in the single-currency area. The EU's evolution began in postwar western Europe, and it has only slowly accommodated new

---

* The fines are not automatically imposed, and the language of the treaty is not as strong as many make it out to be. If a country is in recession characterized by a four-quarter fall in GDP of over 2.0 percent, it receives an automatic exemption. If GDP falls by any amount between 0.75 and 2.0 percent, then only a majority vote by the EU's board of economics and finance ministers (a.k.a. ECOFIN) can impose a fine. Even if GDP falls by less than 0.75 percent, fines will be imposed only "as a rule." The logic behind such weak language is that government budget deficits help countries to "spend their way out" of recessions. Imposing a massive fine on a lagging economy may only make matters worse, aggravating regional instability.

members. Though many east European nations would like to join the EU, strict requirements concerning democratic institutions, economic stability, free trade, and human rights have precluded membership.

Switzerland and Norway are also outside of the euro zone because neither is a member of the European Union. Both countries have long traditions of nonalignment. Switzerland's tradition of independence and neutrality stretches as far back as 1815. Swiss voters even rejected a parliamentary proposal to join the United Nations in 1986. Only time will tell if economic pressures (over 60 percent of Swiss exports go to the EU) will push Switzerland to join in the future.

Greece is not part of monetary union because it didn't meet the convergence criteria defined by the Treaty on European Union (see previous question). With a 1997 inflation rate of 5.2 percent, a long-term interest rate of 9.8 percent, and a budget deficit of 4.0 percent, it didn't clear the required economic hurdles. Greece has indicated that it hopes to qualify by 2001, but many experts claim that this is unlikely.

Great Britain, Denmark, and Sweden meet the convergence criteria but currently do not want to participate. Public opinion in those countries is highly fractured, and leading political parties are hostile to the euro. The British, for instance, have long prided themselves on independence from the rest of the continent and, with a booming economy during 1997–1998, saw little benefit from joining monetary union. When Britain signed the Treaty on European Union in 1992, it negotiated a specific "opt-out right" that allows it to forgo the euro but still be a member of the EU. England's reigning Labor Party has announced that the country will join monetary union only after a national referendum on the issue. A clear majority of British businesses favor EMU, though many special-interest groups are staunchly opposed.

In Denmark, voters are generally unsupportive of European unification and specifically opposed to the euro. The first Danish referendum on joining the European Union failed. The second, in 1993, passed only after the European Commission penciled another opt-out right into the Treaty, this time for Denmark. If Denmark does join monetary union in the future, its political parties may choose to do so only after a national referendum on the issue.

In Sweden, sharp political disagreement over the euro has fractured the major political parties and left public sentiment toward the euro somewhat hostile. Neutral during the two world wars and generally nonaligned in times of peace, Swedes tend to view international alliances with skepticism. Sweden didn't even join the European Union until 1995. The country does not have an official "opt-out" clause written into the Treaty on European Union, as do England and Denmark, but it has used convergence criteria technicalities to justify nonparticipation for the time being.

7. Can other countries join the single-currency zone in the future?

The 11 founding members of the euro zone may have company in the near future. Any EU country that fulfills the convergence criteria may join the euro zone, and there is no preset limit on the number of countries that can ultimately participate. In fact, the Treaty on European Union stipulates that every two years, or upon the request of a member state, the European Council shall determine which EU members fulfill the conditions necessary to join monetary union.

There is no doubt that the euro will continue to be the subject of vociferous political debates in Great Britain, Denmark, Sweden, and Greece. If the euro's launch in 1999 runs smoothly, these countries may see national referendums on the issue in the next five years, though none of the three legally requires one. Great Britain has already indicated that it is likely to join in 2002.

Euroland may also grow as a result of EU expansion. Ten central and eastern European nations have already been invited to join the EU. Five of these—the Czech Republic, Estonia, Hungary, Poland, and Slovenia—are on a fast-track integration process that may result in membership as early as 2002. It will be many years before any of these 10 countries fulfill the convergence criteria (and therefore are allowed to adopt the euro), but EU acceptance is likely to launch the same round of fiscal belt-tightening and budget reform in these countries that dramatically transformed current EU economies between 1992 and 1998. Since four of the five fast-track candidates send more than half of their total exports to the EU, the incentives for reform are enormous.

Chapter Summary

- The euro is the newly created currency of the European Union. Over the next few years, it will completely replace the Austrian schilling, Belgian franc, Finnish markka, French franc, German mark, Irish punt, Italian lira, Luxembourg franc, Dutch guilder, Portuguese escudo, and Spanish peseta.

- The euro is being introduced in three distinct phases. Phase A began on May 1, 1998, when the European Council announced that 11 of the European Union's 15 member countries would introduce the euro. Phase B started on January 1, 1999, and is predominately characterized by the use of the euro as "book money."

Phase C will start on January 1, 2002. At that time, euro notes and coins will appear for the first time.

- The new currency is denominated in bills of 5, 10, 20, 50, 100, 200, and 500 euros; coins of 1 or 2 euros; and coins of 1, 2, 5, 10, 20, and 50 cents. The euro's design was determined by interviews with nearly 2000 taxi drivers, bank cashiers, and retailers and a panel composed of artists, marketers, and communications specialists.

- Economic and Monetary Union has given birth to one of the largest and most powerful trading blocs in the world. In terms of GDP, population, imports, exports, and standard of living, the single European market rivals the United States.

- When EU leaders met in Maastricht to draft the Treaty on European Union, they created specific entrance requirements to be surmounted by any country wishing to participate. These requirements are known as the "convergence criteria," and they were created to ensure that (1) any country joining monetary union is fiscally responsible, and (2) participating countries are sufficiently similar economically to warrant a single monetary policy. In the future, fiscal responsibility will be governed by the Stability & Growth Pact, an agreement that imposes fines on countries that run excessive budget deficits.

- Greece is not part of monetary union because it didn't meet the convergence criteria defined by the Treaty on European Union. Great Britain, Denmark, and Sweden are not participating because voters in those countries are hostile to the euro. Switzerland and Norway are not members of the European Union and therefore not part of the unification process.

- Any EU country that fulfills the convergence criteria may join the euro zone, and there is no preset limit on the number of countries that will ultimately participate. The next few years will bring intense euro-related debates in Great Britain, Denmark, Sweden, and Greece and will likely witness the addition of at least one of those countries to monetary union.

CHAPTER 2

Birth of the Euro

Why have European Union governments invested so much energy in the euro, a project that has consumed 15 nations, countless treaties, and decades of underlying research? Why does the euro go to the heart of Europe's most important economic and business issues, and what are the benefits and risks of launching monetary union? Why do some experts think that the euro will totally collapse, and what ramifications would a breakdown have for the world economy? If the euro is successful, what will it mean?

The purpose of this chapter is to answer these questions and others. In doing so, it presents a brief history of EMU, introduces the major objectives of the project, and describes the key international agreements that now define the most basic terms of Euroland economies. A solid understanding of these issues is essential to analyzing the worldwide significance of the new currency.

8. How did the idea of a single European currency evolve?

The euro is part and parcel of the more general process of European political unification, a process that has captivated political leaders for decades and has often been pursued without regard to economic logic. It began in 1946, when Winston Churchill first called for the creation of a "United States of Europe" that would bring "happiness, prosperity, and glory" to the people of a ravaged continent.[7] His motives were political. He believed that the creation of a single European government would usher in an era of lasting peace to a continent destroyed by two world wars. He believed, with many others, that economic integration precludes armed conflict.

Churchill's idea took root in 1952, when six west European countries created the European Coal and Steel Community (ECSC). Coal and steel were arguably the most important strategic resources of the time, and the ECSC required its creators to delegate their powers over those resources to an independent authority. Despite the economic nature of the agreement, it was primarily designed "to prevent a military conflict between France and Germany"[8] on a continent "long divided by bloody conflict," not necessarily to improve the management of either coal or steel. Foreign observers consequently viewed the ECSC as a harbinger of greater political cooperation.

Their predictions were soon realized. In 1958, France, West Germany, Belgium, the Netherlands, Luxembourg, and Italy ratified the Treaty of Rome, thereby creating the European Economic Community (EEC). The EEC was designed to reduce trade barriers, streamline economic policies, coordinate transportation and agricultural policies, remove measures restricting free competition, and promote the mobility of labor and capital among member nations. It was so successful in stimulating European trade, which quadrupled in value between 1958 and 1968, that plans for new areas of collaboration flourished. But it is important to point out that the Treaty of Rome, despite its economic nature, had considerably more to do with establishing a lasting peace in western Europe than with free market ideology. The EEC was principally designed to launch an "ever closer" and long-term political union among European governments, not just to promote international trade for its own sake. In fact, political integration strengthened still further in 1967, when the Merger Treaty fused the EEC, the ECSC, and European Atomic Energy Community (Euratom) into a larger, more powerful agreement known as the European Community (EC).

In the late 1960s, talk of European political and economic collaboration increasingly began to revolve around exchange rate agreements, partly due to the persistent failure of the Bretton Woods agreements to maintain European currency stability. Created in 1944 by representatives from 44 countries, the Bretton Woods agreements brought about an era of general exchange rate stability that lasted over 20 years. Under the Bretton Woods system, currencies were pegged to the U.S. dollar and allowed to fluctuate only 1 percent above or below predesignated values. Extreme exchange rate fluctuations distort market prices, confuse consumers, hamper international trade, and hinder investment. Hence, the Bretton Woods fixed–exchange rate system played a crucial role in restoring economic growth and stability to Europe in the postwar period.

By the late 1960s, however, Bretton Woods showed increasing signs of weakness. Germany and France devalued the mark and franc, respectively, thereby threatening the stability of other European currencies. Hence, in December of 1969, Luxembourg Prime Minister Pierre Werner was asked to author a high-level EC report on the creation of a complete monetary union among European economies. The Werner Report appeared in 1970, using the term "Economic and Monetary Union" for the first time. The report not only stressed the need for monetary cooperation, but also specifically suggested that the creation of a single European currency could be feasible.

Unfortunately, this early plan for monetary union was foiled by an unexpected event: President Nixon's decision in 1971 to adopt a policy of "benign neglect" toward the U.S. dollar. In short, the United States announced that it was no longer willing to risk its gold reserves for the sake of maintaining Bretton Woods' predefined exchange rates against the dollar. Nixon's decision to "float" the dollar resulted in the collapse of the Bretton Woods system.

Consequently, European leaders put aside the Werner Report and struggled to create a more immediate solution to persistent currency fluctuations. Years of experimentation and negotiation ultimately culminated in the creation of the European Monetary System (EMS) in 1979. (See Figure 2-1.) The EMS

FIGURE 2-1

A brief history of the European Union.

From World War to Monetary Union

1944   Bretton Woods Agreement

Establishes a fixed–exchange rate system among the world's major currencies.

1945   End of World War II

Spurs talk of a "United States of Europe" to end centuries of armed conflict.

1952   European Coal and Steel Community (ECSC)

First major step toward trans-European cooperation. Shows that economic union could be a precursor to political union.

1958   European Economic Community (EEC)

Lays the groundwork for an enormous "common market" for goods and services. Many of its suggestions remain unimplemented for years.

1967   Merger Treaty

Combines the EEC, ECSC, and Euratom into a single international organization known as the European Community (EC). Important step toward consolidating political cooperation on the Continent.

1970   Werner Report

Official EC proposal to create a long-term "Economic and Monetary Union (EMU)."

1971   Collapse of Bretton Woods

Era of fixed exchange rates comes to an end. European leaders put aside the Werner Report and look for a more immediate solution to the problem of currency instability.

1979   European Monetary System

Locks exchange rates among participating nations into narrow, predefined trading zones. Considered an early form of monetary union.

1987   Single European Act

Solidifies, expands, and enforces many of the "common market" ideas first imagined by the original EEC agreements.

F I G U R E 2-1

A brief history of the European Union. (*Continued*)

1989	Delors Report
	Official EC study that recommends the three-stage creation of a single currency.
1990	Stage I of EMU begins
	Involves the final removal of barriers to the movement of goods, services, labor, and capital in the European Union.
1992	European Union (EU)
	Deepest and broadest cooperation agreement ever created. The European Community (EC), as well as the EMU project, become part of the EU.
1994	Stage II of EMU begins
	Creation of the European Monetary Institute and the announcement of which countries would participate in the single-currency zone.
1999	Stage III of EMU begins
	First appearance of the euro as legal currency, though only as "book money."

The European Union: Who Joined When?

1958	France, West Germany, Belgium, the Netherlands, Luxembourg, and Italy
1973	Denmark, Ireland, and the United Kingdom
1981	Greece
1986	Spain and Portugal
1995	Austria, Finland, and Sweden

featured an exchange rate mechanism (ERM) that restricted the movement of EC currencies (except those of the United Kingdom, Spain, and Portugal, who initially declined to participate) to narrow predefined trading bands known as a *parity grid*. This was an early and generally successful form of monetary union.

Though the EMS agreement did not create a single currency, it "locked" participating currencies into predictable trading zones, which in turn promoted economic stability.

Although efforts to expand European political cooperation slowed during the collapse of Bretton Woods and the creation of the European Monetary System, they were rejuvenated in the 1980s. Stagnant economic growth galvanized years of negotiations in this period, ultimately leading to the Single European Act of 1987, an act which promised to systematically remove any border checks, tariffs, customs, and capital and labor restrictions that still remained after decades of efforts to unify European economies. Its objective was the completion of an unrestricted common market by the end of 1992. It began with the elimination of barriers to banking, securities, insurance, and other financial services.

Shortly after the EC passed the Single European Act, Jacques Delors, then president of the European Commission, published a crucial report that revisited the idea of Economic and Monetary Union (EMU). Like the Werner Report many years before it, the 1989 Delors Report presented a specific three-stage plan for implementing monetary union calling for the creation of a single trans-European currency. The Delors Report was extremely well received, both by those who thought integration was the best way to produce a lasting peace in Europe and by those committed to the purely economic benefits of free trade and stable exchange rates. Many observers viewed the euro as the best way to cement 40 years of international cooperation into place, because the introduction of a single currency is by nature irreversible. Once national currencies and monetary policies are destroyed, it is nearly impossible to bring them back.

The EC launched the monetary unification project almost immediately after the publication of the Delors Report. Stage one of EMU began in July of 1990 and had the same general goals as the Single European Act: to ensure that all restrictions on the movement of goods, services, labor, and capital were permanently eliminated. When European heads of state subsequently gathered in Maastricht to found the European Union in 1992, the EMU project became one part of the EU, and specific plans for the second and third stages of the process were drawn up.

Stage two started on January 1, 1994, and was characterized by the establishment of the European Monetary Institute (EMI), which would later become the European Central Bank. The EMI used Stage two to draft strategic and operational plans for a single monetary policy and to help determine which countries were economically "fit" to join a single-currency area. Stage two also witnessed the first use of the word *euro*. Before the Madrid Summit of 1995, the new currency had been known around the world as the "ecu." Stage three then began on January 1, 1999. On that date, almost three decades after the Werner Report first suggested the concept, the euro became the official currency of 11 nations.

9. Why is the European Union creating the euro?

The most common misconception among new observers of monetary union is the belief that the euro is fundamentally an *economic* project. In fact, as the answer to the previous question suggests, the euro is an intensely *political* project that has been deeply entangled in European history for many years. Put simply, the euro has evolved as an essential step toward the ultimate goal of "ever closer" political integration first outlined in the 1958 Treaty of Rome, and the language of subsequent treaties makes it clear that the euro's introduction is based on far more than calculations of economic pros and cons. In fact, Helmut Kohl, former chancellor of Germany and one of the most outspoken proponents of monetary union, views the euro's economic benefits as secondary, instead emphasizing that "The bitter experiences of war and dictatorship in this century teach us that the unification project is the best insurance against a relapse of national egoism, chauvinism and violent conflict."[9] Even today, the legacy of two world wars plays a crucial role in the process of European integration.

There are other political motivations. Ireland views the euro as a means of reducing its reputation as an offshoot of England. Italy wants to avoid becoming a political pariah. France desperately wants to diminish its susceptibility to the monetary policy decisions of the Germans. Many enthusiastic German leaders hope monetary union will be the "cart" that drags the "horse" of total political union. Indeed, there are now as many justifications for the euro as there are participating countries, because each EU nation perceives a particular set of advantages and risks.

Although the euro is the child of a wide range of political agendas, ambitious economic goals have played an important, if secondary, role since the very beginning. Clearly, political solidarity in Europe would hardly be furthered if the euro's creators believed that the new currency rested on feeble economic footing. In fact, in the midst of political diversity, high-minded economic objectives have emerged as the most common answers to the "Why are they doing this?" question. According to the 1970 Werner Report, in which EMU was first formally proposed, "[Monetary] union will make it possible to ensure growth and stability within the Community and reinforce the contribution it can make to economic and monetary equilibrium in the world and make it a pillar of stability." The 1992 Treaty on European Union itself cited "the raising of the standard of living and the quality of life, and economic and social cohesion and solidarity among Member States" as its central goal.

But why are European leaders convinced that a single currency is a boon to economic stability and growth? Such sweeping objectives, noble and uncontroversial, beg the immediate question as to how they may be achieved. The answer warrants a careful look at the specific benefits of creating a common currency.

10. What are the euro's core economic advantages?

Exchange rate risk. In the international business environment, decisions made today are often adversely affected by future shifts in exchange rates. When Germany's BMW invests $100 million to augment its French sales force, its estimation of the investment's profitability pivots on the expected exchange rate between the German mark and the French franc. If the franc were to sharply depreciate after the investment, then the sales of BMWs in France (collected in francs) suddenly translate into fewer marks for the parent company in Munich, making the investment significantly less attractive or even unprofitable. Hence, the more unpredictable are exchange rates, the more risky are foreign investments and the less likely companies are to pursue growth in foreign markets. The euro, by virtue of replacing national currencies like the mark and franc, completely eliminates exchange rate risk between participating currencies. This will be a boon to international investment in Euroland.

Exchange rate risk is potentially troublesome to any consumer, producer, or investor who makes an economic decision today that results in a payoff, or the delivery of a good or service, at a later date. Unfortunately, this describes the vast majority of economic activities. Consider the Belgian manu-

facturer who builds a plant in Portugal that takes 12 months to
finish. Or an Irish investor who buys stock in an Italian services
firm based on a promising five-year business plan. In fact, even
the most mundane corporate purchases are characterized by
separate order, delivery, and payment dates, leaving firms constantly exposed to exchange rate risk. Figure 2-2, which shows
the contribution of exports to EU economies, demonstrates just
how important unimpaired cross-border trade is to European
growth. (Note that Figure 2-2*a* and *b* shows the same information in two different formats.)

FIGURE 2-2a

A continent built on exports.

Country	Exports as a Percentage of GDP
Germany	30%
Belgium	84%
Netherlands	63%
France	29%
Italy	28%
Spain	30%
Portugal	43%
Austria	49%
Ireland	84%
Finland	37%
UK	32%
Greece	19%
Sweden	47%
Denmark	41%

Source: Eurostat.

FIGURE 2-2b

A continent built on exports. (*Continued*)

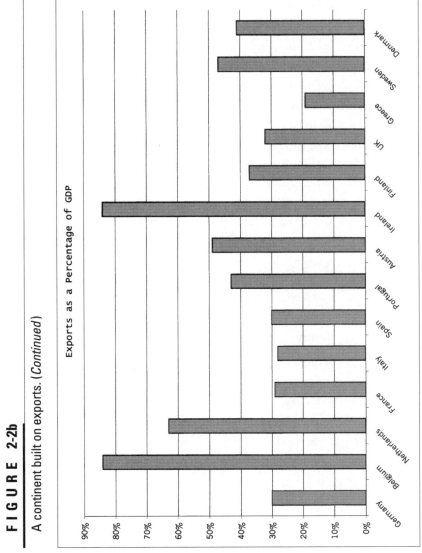

Exports as a Percentage of GDP

Though hedging techniques certainly exist, they are not a sufficient solution to the problem. Firms constantly hedge their risk through the foreign exchange futures markets, in which they buy the right to exchange foreign currencies in the future for the rate that prevails today. But hedging has a price, just as any insurance policy has a price. It's not free, and may be as high as 2 percent of small firms' sales and purchases.[10] More important, hedging instruments are not available to every business, particularly not to small, illiquid firms and companies in countries with immature futures markets (e.g., Ireland, Spain, and Portugal).

Transaction costs. Tourists planning European excursions before the euro encumbered themselves with the hassle and cost of many currencies, each recognized by a small geographic segment of the European Union—and exchangeable only through banks, *bureaux de change,* traveler service offices, and credit card companies for a fee. These fees present themselves in the form of fixed commissions (say, 1 percent) as well as in the spread between the buying and selling prices of any given currency. One study estimates that the average tourist pays roughly $13 in such currency conversion costs with every European border crossing, a cost that burdens tens of millions of such trips per year.[11] The euro eliminates these costs.

Yet the tourism industry offers only one modest example of the euro's transaction-cost savings. The economic heartbeat of Euroland encompasses tens of thousands of cross-currency transactions every day. Austrian manufacturing firms sell parts to clients in the Netherlands, France, and Italy, which in turn sell their wares in Portugal and Spain. The majority of such cross-border sales involve currency conversion costs, usually conducted through large financial institutions.

It is difficult to estimate exactly how large the euro's transaction-cost savings will ultimately be, but for Europe, a continent in which international trade is vitally important, the savings will be substantial. One European Commission study estimates that, before the euro, European businesses converted $7.7 trillion per year from one EU currency to another, paying $12.8 billion in conversion charges, or 0.4 percent of European Union GDP.[12] Such costs are particularly acute for firms in small countries with illiquid foreign exchange markets and unsophisticated banking systems.

Price transparency. A single currency makes price differences between goods, services, and wages in different countries more evident, thus enhancing competition across markets. In the absence of the euro, Euroland consumers found it difficult and tiresome to compare the prices of computers, appliances, building materials, automobiles, consulting services, or general contractors across national boundaries. Germans, for example, were unaccustomed to thinking in "thousands of lira" and Italians found the Portuguese escudo intangible and distant. As a result, price discrimination was easily implemented. In 1997, an Audi A4 cost about 38,000 marks in Germany, but only 27,000 in Denmark; a Fiat Barchetta cost about 37,200 marks in Germany and 28,000 in Italy.[13]

But euro prices provide a simple and consistent platform for comparison, spurring households and businesses across the continent to compare prices abroad. Price discrimination in everything from Audi A4s to candy bars is now considerably more difficult than it was before the euro. Due to the absence of exchange rate risk, entrepreneurs feel more comfortable establishing businesses that take advantage of small differences in cross-border prices. This, in turn, is leading to price equalization across borders.

This idea, however, shouldn't be taken too far. Some observers claim that the euro will eliminate continental price differences for identical goods and services: "A bottle of Coca-

Cola in Belgium will have to cost the same as in France."[14] Such claims are totally inaccurate. Prices are determined by the complex interaction of supply, demand, and regulation in a wide variety of competitive environments. The introduction of a common currency does not *eliminate* price differences in Euroland anymore than the U.S. dollar establishes a common price for a can of Coke between Maine and Arizona.

Deep financial markets. Before the euro, efforts to match the immediate financial needs of consumers with the investment requirements of savers were plagued by the psychological and economic costs of 11 national currencies. Every type of financial instrument, from government bonds and commercial bank loans to common stock and high-risk derivatives, was listed in a national denomination. This fractured the financial markets and discouraged foreign investment—and would have done so even in the absence of transaction costs and exchange rate risk. Imagine the headaches that would plague Wall Street investors if U.S. stocks were priced in individual state currencies (California dollars, Delaware dollars, etc.).

The euro revolutionizes this situation. Since January 1, 1999, Euroland's major exchanges have listed their financial instruments, including those previously issued, in euros. Austrian investment funds now invest in euro-denominated bonds from the Italian government without the psychological and economic impact of currency conversions and foreign price quotes. German banks offer a single financial product, euro loans, to companies throughout the European Union. To investors and borrowers alike, such developments have made the European financial markets broader, more accessible, and more liquid. Because this promotes unrestricted international trade in the world's single most important market—the market for money itself—it is considered one of the euro's core economic benefits.

11. What larger economic goals does the European Union hope the euro will achieve?

The euro's core economic benefits (eliminating exchange rate risk, reducing transaction costs, increasing price transparency, and deepening financial markets) follow inevitably from the act of replacing the mark, schilling, markka, franc, krona, guilder, peseta, punt, lira, and escudo with a single means of payment. But the euro also offers a host of *indirect* economic advantages. These benefits hinge on deeper changes in the behavior of financial markets and firms and are, as a result, more controversial.

Macroeconomic stability.   Many of the European Union's 15 member countries, including some of EMU's first-round participants, have battled inflation since World War II. Ireland, England, Italy, Portugal, and Spain have been particularly susceptible to inflation, a phenomenon that confuses buyers and sellers, increases borrowing costs, raises the effective tax rate, sends negative signals to investors, and creates gross market inefficiencies (see question 17).

But the euro introduces a new regime of low inflation and macroeconomic stability for many Euroland countries. According to some experts, this is virtually guaranteed because Euroland now possesses the most independent central bank in the world, the European Central Bank (ECB). Central banks "steer" a country's inflation rate by using a variety of monetary policy instruments to lower or raise the general level of demand (see question 21). The more independent a central bank, the less likely it is to succumb to the political pressures of its government to allow an economy to grow too fast or to finance excessive public expenditures. Politicians and central bankers are often at odds with one another, because central banks are more interested in long-term stability than in short-term economic gain. Indeed, research shows that greater central bank independence leads to lower inflation.

Yet history has shown that the central banks of many Euroland countries are not immune from political influence. That is precisely why the euro may be a boon to long-term regional stability. As one economist puts it, "The European central bank . . . will be the first central bank in history without a government looking over its shoulder."[15] The ECB is also closely modeled after the German Bundesbank, an institution known worldwide for its tradition of independence. Although the ECB's high level of independence brings little to countries already known for low inflation (Germany, Austria, Belgium, and the Netherlands), it promises a more stable economic future for the others. Italians, for instance, view price stability as one of the euro's primary benefits.

Lower interest rates. To the extent that the euro lowers inflation, it also exerts downward pressure on interest rates. Investors buy bonds only if they are sure that the money they receive in the future will result in a percentage return that is higher than the inflation rate. Investors consequently demand lower interest rates, or "inflation premiums," from countries with greater price stability. This benefit is particularly important for countries with poor inflation-fighting records (Italy, Spain, and Portugal). These countries now benefit from reduced inflation expectations because of the stringent goals and determination of the new European Central Bank.

The euro also brings lower interest rates by reducing exchange rate risk (see question 10). In the past, an investor in Luxembourg wanting to buy an Irish government bond demanded extra interest to compensate him or her for the risk of losing money through changes in the punt-franc exchange rate. This extra interest, called the *exchange rate risk premium,* is now eliminated on international debt transactions that occur within Euroland. According to one economist, the benefit of reducing exchange rate risk premiums on interest rates could, for Europe's weaker currencies, "be equivalent to reducing real long-term interest rates by perhaps two percentage points or more, and this would represent a substantial and permanent reduction in the cost of capital in those economies."[16] It is crucial to point out, however, that countries with a history of low interest rates (e.g., Germany, Austria and the Netherlands) are not likely to be helped by the euro in this regard.

Structural reform.   Some experts argue that the euro encourages badly needed structural reform in Europe. In short, countries wishing to qualify for the euro had to push their economies into shape by meeting the convergence criteria set forth in the Treaty on European Union (see question 5). In the future, they must adhere to the Stability & Growth Pact, an agreement that strictly limits government borrowing and forces governments to shape up their public finances. The pact even *fines* countries that borrow too much.

Such measures have raised fundamental questions about the long-term feasibility of many of Europe's notoriously large public spending and welfare programs. In particular, they have resulted in major budget cuts and have placed renewed attention on the importance of sustainable economic growth. Budget tightening in countries like Portugal resulted in sharp declines in interest rates very early on in the process, as financial markets reassessed what had previously been viewed as a financially irresponsible government. This in turn sparked a prolonged economic boom in that country that continues today. It is for precisely this reason that the U.S. government has strongly endorsed the euro's effect on structural reform from across the Atlantic, saying that the euro is modernizing European economies, shrinking the size of their welfare states, and encouraging a modern, global view.[17]

Reserve currency status. EU leaders hope that the euro will become a major international reserve currency. Reserve currencies are used by central banks, governments, and private firms worldwide as a long-term store of value and to meet their ongoing financial requirements. The dollar is currently the world's premiere reserve currency, adorning the vaults of central banks and major financial institutions from Tokyo to Caracas. Although the United States accounts for less than 20 percent of world trade, the dollar is used in about 83 percent[18] of two-way foreign exchange transactions and comprises 63 percent of official currency reserves worldwide.[19] Historically speaking, only currencies that are highly liquid, stable, and accepted as payment in a large economic area have the potential to become major reserve currencies.

But why are EU leaders so anxious to establish a major reserve currency? Put simply, they are aware of the tremendous advantages that the dollar's status in global finance brings to the U.S. economy. Reserve currencies are highly demanded and therefore benefit from high liquidity and extremely low transaction costs in foreign exchange markets. This is a multimillion-dollar boon, for instance, to U.S. businesses that convert foreign revenue into dollars. Reserve currency status similarly benefits a nation's securities markets, because buyers interested in holding a reserve currency buy assets denominated in that currency. This in turn lowers the cost of borrowing for firms and governments raising money in that currency. The U.S. government, for instance, has long been able to finance its trade deficits by borrowing extremely cheaply from abroad. Enormous worldwide demand for dollar investments makes borrowing easy. Indeed, EU leaders have been very public about their envy of this "exorbitant privilege" for decades and hope to benefit similarly. Reserve currency status also saves the United States billions of dollars in direct conversion costs, because the dollar is accepted as payment around the world. The majority of the world's oil sales, for instance, occur in U.S. dollars, even when such transactions occur between Saudi Arabia and Germany.

Economic growth.   Lower transaction costs and exchange rate risk, coupled with price transparency and a single means of payment, have increased the effective size of product markets across Euroland. As a result, some argue that multinationals can now achieve economies of scale (i.e., the ability to produce products at a lower average cost than competitors due to high volume) never before seen in European business environments. Economic historians know that economies of scale have been a key determinant of the United States' industrial success for centuries. Euroland now hopes to benefit from the lower average costs, higher productivity, and enhanced competitiveness promised by a large internal market. This will be made even more certain, they say, because the European Central Bank brings stable prices and lower interest rates.

The upshot of all this, claim many politicians, is that the euro will deliver Europe to a golden age of *higher economic growth.* Some economists, including the president of the European Central Bank, have predicted that the euro may ultimately increase economic growth in the EU up to 1 percent per year.[20] Others put the figure even higher, a shocking result considering a growth difference between the United States and England of around 2 percent was enough to transform the United States from a postcolonial agrarian state into the world's most powerful economy between 1820 and 1870.[21] Small wonder, then, that the pursuit of monetary union has occupied the minds of politicians and economists for decades.

12. What are the costs of introducing the euro?

Though the euro promises substantial economic advantages, it also brings many costs. These costs have served as penetrating ammunition for the euro's critics, and they resulted in the near collapse of the project prior to 1999.

Transition costs.   Between 1999 and 2002, public and private institutions worldwide will spend billions of dollars to adjust invoices, price lists, price tags, office forms, payrolls, bank accounts, databases, keyboards, software programs, vending machines, ATMs, parking meters, phone booths, postage meters, and counting machines, to name only a few items, to a new currency. Production of the euro notes and coins themselves is costing billions of dollars. Computerized parking meters require up to $800 each to reconfigure.[22] Harder to measure, but equally important, are the countless training and disruption costs of making euro transitions. The consulting firm KPMG estimates that the total transition cost will ultimately come to about $50 billion for Europe's largest companies, with an average cost of around $30 million per company.[23] Other studies place the worldwide cost at close to 1 percent of Euroland's total GDP.[24]

Job losses.   Currency traders and analysts in Frankfurt and Paris are wondering where their income will come from once EMU is fully completed. Price Waterhouse estimates that some banks could lose up to 50 percent of their foreign exchange business and 60 percent of their revenue from bond arbitrage trading. The creation of a single currency simply obviates the need for many cross-currency transactions and hedging instruments. One analyst estimates that the euro will eliminate $350 billion in daily foreign exchange volume, about 22 percent of the world's foreign exchange market.[25] *Bureaux de change* are clear losers in EMU, losing perhaps

$1.9 billion, or two-thirds of their business, by 2010.[26] Of course, some of these job losses are being made up by gains in industries associated with the introduction of the euro, such as those involved with software and office machines. Yet it is clear that the sheer magnitude of EMU poses a painful threat to many professions.

Opportunity costs. Any serious analysis of the euro's overarching pros and cons must consider the tremendous effort devoted to developing the project by local, regional, national, and international governments, as well as the countless hours of analysis and preparation required by the private sector. Critics of the euro argue that such resources, billions of dollars' worth, would have been better spent reforming Europe's troubling structural problems, such as those stemming from unemployment, unsustainable public welfare programs, skewed taxation systems, stagnant innovation, or ineffective privatization. Although it is impossible to measure the euro's total opportunity cost, all parties agree that the investment has been enormous.

13. What are the two major risks that could disrupt, or even destroy, the euro's success?

Despite their tremendous size, the euro's implementation costs are marginal compared to the two major *ongoing* risks of monetary union. The ongoing risks are not one-time costs that will soon disappear. Rather, they will threaten the sustainability of the euro for decades to come. Although these risks are somewhat complex, understanding them is an absolutely crucial element of comprehending the new trans-European economy.

Economic shocks. Economic shocks are unexpected changes in the macroeconomic environment of a country or region that disrupt the careful balance of production, consumption, investment, government spending, and trade. The most threatening type of economic shock for the single-currency area is known as an *asymmetric shock,* so called because such shocks affect countries unequally. They can be caused by sharp declines or increases in demand for the primary goods and services of a specific country. When world demand for forest products ebbs, for instance, the economic health of Finland deteriorates much more severely and quickly than that of Austria, France, or Luxembourg, because forest products make up an enormous portion of Finland's GDP. Similarly, when world demand for wine and tourism declines sharply, France is hit much harder than Finland, Belgium, or the Netherlands. The common feature of such scenarios is that economic growth in one country slows while that in surrounding countries does not.*

Before the arrival of the euro, Euroland countries could handle asymmetric shocks—and the recessions that often follow them—in three primary ways: interest rate adjustment, exchange rate intervention, and fiscal adjustment. Of these, interest rate adjustment was the most important. For decades, Finland's central bank responded to economic downturns (such as those caused by sagging demand in the forestry industry) by lowering Finnish interest rates. This in turn lowered the cost of borrowing, which spurred industrial investment and consumption, ultimately renewing economic growth in that country. Such a transition—from interest rate changes to renewed growth—is the hallmark of monetary policy in every industrialized country of the world and is a pivotal mechanism for responding to economic downturns.

---

* It's worth pointing out that economic shocks can be caused by a variety of factors. Changes in aggregate demand, commodity prices, or productivity trends can create economic divergence among nations. Also, economic shocks needn't be negative shocks. Economic divergence can occur, for instance, when one nation booms while its neighbors grow modestly.

The euro, however, makes independent interest rate adjustments impossible, because Euroland's national central banks surrendered monetary policy authority to the European Central Bank in Frankfurt as of January 1, 1999. There is now a single set of short-term interest rates for all euro participants. Hence, unless economic shocks hit all 11 countries simultaneously, and with roughly equal magnitude, interest rate adjustments cannot be used to manage them.

The second major way in which economies recover from asymmetric shocks is through exchange rate adjustments. Just as the Bank of Finland, before the euro, could manipulate interest rates in order to respond to economic downturns, it could also manipulate exchange rates. By selling large quantities of markka in the foreign exchange markets, Finland's central bank could, in the face of a national recession, devalue the currency and thus decrease the price of Finnish goods abroad in an extremely efficient manner. This could galvanize demand for Finnish imports worldwide and thus jump-start economic recovery. For this reason, countries across Euroland could use currency devaluation as a way of steering their way out of recessions.

Yet for individual countries, the euro eliminates this monetary policy instrument, because the euro is now the common currency for 11 different countries. There is no "Finnish euro" anymore than there is a "Californian dollar." Hence, currencies can no longer be devalued at the national level.

Another way in which Euroland economies dealt with asymmetric shocks before the euro was through fiscal policy adjustment. In short, when an asymmetric shock sends a country into recession, government spending generally increases, because unemployment and social welfare costs rise during hard times. At the same time, government tax receipts decrease, because fewer people are working and wages stagnate. In effect, then, governments go into debt during difficult economic times so that they can spend more money on social programs. Such spending simultaneously introduces massive amounts of money into an economy, spurring consumption and economic growth once again and urging an economy out of recession.

Yet the euro introduces severe restraints on such fiscal stabilizers, because participants must adhere to the new Stability & Growth Pact, an agreement that requires all Euroland government budget deficits to be less than 3.0 percent of GDP (see question 5). The pact was introduced to ensure the long-term economic health and credibility of the euro by preventing nations from borrowing too much. One consequence of this pact, however, is that Euroland governments are now unable or unwilling to allow their public spending to significantly increase during downturns for fear of exceeding the Stability & Growth Pact limit. Hence, another important cure for asymmetric shocks no longer exists.

It appears, then, that the euro has three primary impacts on the ability of countries to respond to asymmetric shocks: it precludes independent interest rate movements; it prevents currency devaluations; and it restricts the ability of government spending to stabilize an economy. It is the combination of these three factors that poses the biggest ongoing threat to the euro and prompts Europe's most pressing economic question: Can individual Euroland economies respond to asymmetric economic shocks without the monetary and fiscal flexibility that they had before the euro? As Nobel Laureate Milton Friedman writes, "Whether [a common currency] is good or bad depends primarily on the adjustment mechanisms that are available to absorb the economic shocks and dislocations that impinge on the entities considering such a currency."[27] He concludes that the euro is not, in fact, a good idea. The underlying fear is that some countries—like Finland in the preceding example—will soon enter recessions and be unable to escape them in any reasonable period of time. Its three recession-fighting tools are no longer available.

But doesn't the United States suffer from the same risks? The United States manages to maintain a monetary union between 50 widespread states without independent interest rate changes and currency devaluations and without massive annual budget deficits. Is it really fair to say that asymmetric shocks pose a grave threat to Euroland when they don't to the United States?

Though it is true that U.S. states are also susceptible to asymmetric shocks, the United States is different than the European Union in several profound ways. First, the United States is home to the most flexible labor markets in the world. When demand for U.S. automobiles collapses, Michigan's economy, which is heavily centered in that industry, rapidly deteriorates even while the economies of its neighboring states may boom. But Michigan manages to recover from its recession because the United States has a high degree of *labor mobility.* As jobs in the automobile industry are cut and wages sink, workers pack up and move to areas and industries with stronger economic growth. This provides a new pool of skilled labor to Michigan's neighbors, thus channeling inexpensive labor resources to the industries that need them. These labor movements simultaneously reduce unemployment in Michigan and lessen the number of people that the flagging automobile industry must support. In essence, labor mobility conditions economic renewal.

Yet the European labor force is nowhere near as flexible. Labor mobility stems naturally from common language and culture, and the European Union is home to 11 official languages and 15 very different societies. Where the United States shares a unifying language, a single government, an enormous and homogeneous middle class, and a common cultural history, European nations remain fractured and disparate. The average American considers him- or herself first an American and only then a Virginian or Californian, while the average Frenchman or Spaniard pays little or no patriotic regard to the European Union. The natural fallout of this is that only about 5 million of the Europe Union's 370 million citizens live outside their country of birth, and only 3.1 million work in another EU state.[28] Even within countries, labor mobility in Europe remains two to three times lower than that in the United States.[29] It is no wonder, then, that labor market inflexibility contributes to the ongoing risk posed by economic shocks in Euroland.

The European Union is less capable than the United States of recovering from economic shocks for a second reason: its *lack of a fiscal transfer system.* In short, the single central government in the United States is capable of transferring enormous sums of money between its states. Consider an economic downturn in the automobile industry once again. While Detroit hits the skids and heads for recession, other U.S. states continue to grow. California, for instance, may witness incredible growth in the technology, defense, and agriculture sectors while Michigan's economy falters. Consequently, the sales and income tax *receipts* that the U.S. government collects from California increase (because the state is booming) while those collected from Michigan fall (because the state is in recession). Yet U.S. government *expenditures* also change. Michigan begins to receive billions of dollars in unemployment, welfare, and special social program transfers from the U.S. government because of the high unemployment following a recession. But California's receipts from the U.S. government remain relatively constant or may even sink. Hence, California finds itself contributing a greater percentage to the national budget than it used to and receiving a smaller percentage. In Michigan, the opposite occurs. In a way, then, healthy California tax revenue foots the bill for Michigan's downturn. This system of fiscal transfers, which occur through the U.S. government, is a powerful and efficient tool for stabilizing economic differences between U.S. states—such as those caused by economic shocks.

The European Union, however, lacks an effective international fiscal transfer system. In the United States, the federal government raises about twice as much as its state and local governments combined. In Euroland, most taxes are paid to national and local governments. This leaves the European Commission in Brussels with an annual budget of only 2.5 percent of that controlled by the national governments,[30] or 1.27 percent of EU GDP. And about half of this budget, in any case, is dedicated to agricultural policies alone. Although western Germany pays billions of marks to Germany's eastern states through its famous "solidarity tax," and rich northern Italy indirectly subsidizes the much poorer southern end of that country, only very small fiscal transfers occur between Euroland nations. Moreover, the chances that such transfers will increase in the future are slim, because continental politicians who propose large fiscal transfers to other countries sign political death warrants. For this reason, the euro carries the significant risk that fiscal transfers will be unable to cope with the dangerous economic disparities that follow asymmetric shocks.

Political discord. There is a second major ongoing risk to monetary union, apart from that posed by economic shocks. It stems from the fact that European political integration is still in its infancy. The lack of a unified and powerful "European federal government" poses two significant threats to the euro, apart from the fiscal transfer problems just mentioned. The first is that member governments may become financially profligate, thereby endangering the viability of a single currency. The daily spending habits of the 11 first-round participants are not directly controlled by any single authority. Hence, rogue nations may exceed the annual budget deficits outlined in the Stability & Growth Pact without notice, refuse to pay their specified fines, and become political "outsiders" to the rest of the Union. In this way, fiscally conservative and stable countries may be hurt by the excessive borrowing of others, because the excess demands on the capital market of a heavy borrower push up the cost of borrowing for everyone else borrowing in euros, even though distinct national interest rates still exist.[31] It also introduces the risk that a member government may become insolvent, a risk that would unnerve financial markets and thereby destabilize all Euroland economies.

Pursuing an economic union without a strong political union is also risky because severe political tensions may undermine economic cooperation. The president speaks for the United States of America, but who speaks for Europe? The absence of a strong political union introduces the risk that controversial issues, stemming from such factors as NATO expansion, nuclear disarmament, or border disagreements, will fracture the EU. Regional tensions of this kind could plague European economic policy meetings, disrupt financial markets, spark nationalism, and place Euroland's commitment to stability and growth in question, events that would damage the euro's long-term credibility for all participants. Imagine if Germany, in the midst of a political dispute, suddenly banned French wine imports. Or if Spain unilaterally closed its borders to Portuguese passports. Some experts have taken this line of thinking to an extreme, arguing that the euro is bound to "divide Europe like nothing else since 1945."[32] Similar events are highly unlikely in the United States, with its strong federal government, single foreign policy, and shared political history.

14. Do the euro's advantages outweigh its disadvantages?

Despite some general pessimism over the euro's costs and risks, it would seem that the answer to this question is a profound *yes*. Why? Because the euro is, after all, here. It is no longer a theoretical symbol of unity existing only in the minds of a few ambitious politicians. The euro officially came into being on January 1, 1999, under the full leadership and support of 11 heads of state, thousands of politicians, and hundreds of prominent economists. It seems, then, that after careful reflection, Euroland governments determined that the euro's incredible economic promise exceeds its costs and risks.

Unfortunately, the answer is not so simple. No one knows whether the euro's long-term advantages outweigh the risks posed by economic shocks and political instability. As one senior Bundesbank economist points out, "The euro is not about a cost-benefit analysis." The pure political goal of a united and integrated Europe has been the driving force of the euro's creation since the very beginning (see question 9). Economic pros and cons were never the sole focus of attention. And in any case, measuring the euro's millionfold economic effects across the continent is a matter of crude estimation. An accurate cost-benefit analysis of the euro couldn't be completed even if tremendous resources were mustered for the purpose.

The great gamble that the European Union has taken is that the euro's economic opportunities outweigh the risks posed by economic shocks and political discord. Unfortunately, this is a gamble whose outcome won't be determined until the next big economic downturn. It is precisely the seriousness of this gamble, and the stakes involved, that makes EMU one of the most exciting economic events of recent history.

15. Could the euro totally collapse?

Public and private reports on the euro have made reference to "the complete collapse of Economic and Monetary Union" ever since the idea was invented. References to such things as "euro angst" and "currency chaos" continue to haunt the pages of the financial press. Not surprisingly, many European firms have quietly developed contingency scenarios for a post-1999 euro catastrophe.

But is a complete breakdown of the euro still possible? Or are such predictions simply scare tactics employed by longtime opponents of European unification?

The answers depend on who one asks. At the European Central Bank, where copies of the 1992 Treaty on European Union are carried through the corridors like personal bibles, a complete collapse of the euro is "a legal impossibility." This is because nothing in the thousands of pages of treaties, pacts, and official reports published by the European Commission says anything at all about withdrawal from—or the collapse of—monetary union. There is simply no legal framework or allowance for such an event: no special articles, pull-out clauses, extenuating circumstances, or withdrawal requirements.

But it is naive to say that a complete collapse of the euro is impossible simply because it isn't legally sanctioned. Although pessimistic predictions often belie long-term bias against European unification in general, leading economists agree that a collapse of the euro is indeed imaginable. In fact, a majority of euro critics envision the same basic breakdown scenario.

It would all start, they say, with economic divergence among Euroland countries (see question 13). An economic shock caused by a severe recession in the United States, for example, would impact Germany and France, where trade with the United States amounts to an enormous proportion of GDP, much more quickly and severely than it would Luxembourg or Finland.

The direct result of such an economic shock would be a significant worsening of unemployment and investment levels in France and Germany. Because Euroland is characterized by a relatively inflexible labor force and now follows a single monetary policy, countries that fall into recession may have an extremely difficult time reviving their economies and handling unemployment. Normally, the central bank of a country in recession would lower interest rates (i.e., loosen the money supply), in order to encourage consumption and revive economic growth (see question 21). But in this case, other European nations, unhindered by insufficient investment and stagnant growth, would balk at attempts to lower interest rates for fear of sparking inflation in their own countries.

This basic scenario would then give rise to a devastating event: the general public could conceivably lose faith in the euro. George Soros has warned, for example, that the euro will ultimately bear the brunt of European frustration with unemployment, as workers in divergent economies blame the new currency for their troubles. Average unemployment in Euroland already stands at over 11 percent (close to 20 percent in Spain) and has become the region's hottest political issue. Social distrust and unrest could then lead to demonstrations, bank runs, and labor revolts that would push lagging economies into even deeper economic malaise. Political figures espousing anti-euro sentiment would find broad electoral support, a process whose seeds have already been planted (e.g., the National Front in France, the GPU in Germany, and the Freedom Party in Austria). Investors who hadn't already fled from the euro would dump euro holdings en masse.

The combined macroeconomic effect of a national recession, unstable currency markets, labor unrest, and public angst could then force countries to drop out of the euro zone. As one central banker puts it, "Countries could get squeezed and decide to print their own money again." Such a pullout would carry tremendous costs for the entire single-currency area— and for the world economy. Investors know, for example, that any country that pulls out of EMU is likely to witness a massive devaluation of its currency against the euro. But because governments and firms have already issued substantial debt in euros, a devaluation of a national currency would bring the risk of defaults. This in turn would launch a cycle of low investment, economic uncertainty, and prolonged recession. In fact, this is an exact description of the economic malaise that the Asian currency crisis sparked in 1997. In this regard, one point cannot be overstressed: any significant weakening of the European economic zone will have devastating economic effects throughout the world. The 11 participating nations carry too much weight in the world economy to confine a continental recession to their own shores.

Though it would seem, based on this hypothetical scenario, that the euro is extremely vulnerable, the chances of a complete breakdown of the euro are in fact extremely slim. Euroland economies have so far converged much more quickly than anyone thought possible only a few years ago, and they show signs of strong and continued economic growth. Economic shocks are, in fact, extremely rare and do not always result in economic divergence. In any case, it is not clear whether dropping out of the euro zone, even in the case of economic upheaval, would better the situation in an unstable country. It would likely make things worse, providing a powerful incentive to work things out within the euro's institutional framework. Is it likely that the EU would commit collective suicide rather carry out the reforms necessary to ease a crisis situation?[33]

The euro itself was introduced without any significant problems or voter backlash in early 1999, and most economists now agree that the euro has a promising outlook. Moreover, euro breakdown scenarios assume that Euroland's structural rigidities and labor inflexibility will never improve. In the midst of one of the biggest economic transformations Europe has ever seen, such rigidities are waging their own fight for survival.

Chapter Summary

- EMU is best understood as one component of the broader process of European political integration that began in the early 1950s. To this day, the legacy of armed conflict in Europe plays a crucial role in the process of European integration.

- Although the euro is foremost a political project that is deeply entangled in European history, ambitious economic objectives, such as the pursuit of economic growth and the raising of Europe's standard of living, have always played an important, if secondary, role.

- The euro's four core economic benefits are direct and relatively uncontroversial. They are (1) the reduction of transaction costs, (2) the elimination of exchange rate risk, (3) increased price transparency, and (4) the creation of deep financial markets.

- Other economic benefits are more indirect and debatable. They involve (1) macroeconomic stability, (2) lower interest rates, (3) fundamental structural reform, (4) the creation of a new global reserve currency, and (5) increased economic growth.

- The direct costs of implementing the euro are substantial. They consist of (1) transition expenses, (2) job losses, and (3) opportunity costs.

- The ongoing costs and risks of maintaining EMU are less tangible but more serious. They involve the susceptibility to economic shocks and political discord.

- Whether the euro's economic advantages outweigh the risks posed by economic shocks and political instability is unknown. The great gamble that EU leaders have taken is that modern Europe is entering a new era of adaptability and flexibility that ensures the success of monetary union.

- It is naive to say that a complete collapse of the euro is impossible simply because it is not sanctioned by the Treaty on European Union. Nonetheless, the chances of a complete collapse of EMU are extremely slim.

C H A P T E R

Monetary Policy
in the Euro Zone

It is said that Alan Greenspan is the second most powerful man in America. As chairman of the U.S. Federal Reserve ("the Fed"), Greenspan sets the pace of U.S. economic growth and helps shape the ups and downs of world business cycles. Executives, managers, market watchers, analysts, and politicians study his every word in excruciating detail. When the Fed raises or lowers interest rates, markets around the world change with them.

Who will play Greenspan's role in Europe? If the euro is based on the cooperation of 11 different countries, how are interest rates in the single-currency area determined? Doesn't a single currency imply a single central banking system? How are euro exchange rate policies formulated? Why are these issues so important?

By answering these and related questions, this chapter examines the most profound consequence of a single European currency. Put simply, the euro's most important effect is that it completely overturns the structure and operation of monetary policy in 11 of the world's leading economies. An understanding of this transformation is an essential component of understanding the post-euro world, because monetary policy plays a pivotal role in everything from economic growth, inflation, government spending, and exchange rates to industrial investment and export competitiveness. In fact, the euro shakes traditional assumptions on these topics to their foundations.

16. What is the European Central Bank (ECB), and why is it important?

The European Central Bank (ECB) is the highest monetary authority in the euro area. Analogous to the U.S. Federal Reserve, the Bank of Japan, or the German Bundesbank, the ECB is the issuer and constitutional guardian of the euro. Its central activity is to set the critical short-term interest rates that indirectly set the pace of economic growth. As the creator of monetary policy in Euroland, the ECB is the single most important determinant of the euro's ultimate stability and success.

Before the euro's arrival, 11 distinct national central banks formulated monetary policy in Euroland. Each institution, from the German Bundesbank to the Central Bank of Ireland, set national interest rates independently, although formal and informal collaboration existed on many levels. But on January 1, 1999, the ECB inherited exclusive monetary policy authority for Euroland. Now, the 11 national central banks work as subordinate members of a broader central banking system and help the ECB to implement its policies. This system as a whole is known as the European System of Central Banks (ESCB).

The ECB is the institutional successor of the European Monetary Institute (EMI), a term often heard in euro-related discussions. When the European Commission created monetary union, it concluded that it would be best to give birth to a European central bank in stages. Hence, the EMI was founded in 1994 and worked for four years to transform itself into an operating central bank. After much research and debate, it finally succeeded in this task. The EMI officially handed over power to the ECB on June 1, 1998. The ECB is located in the Eurotower in Frankfurt, Germany, and employs about 500 people. It is worth noting, however, that the European System of Central Banks as a whole spans all 11 Euroland countries and employs over 60,000 people.

17. What are the ECB's responsibilities?

Like all central banks, the ECB is the guardian of the currency it issues. But the ECB's mission is defined much more narrowly than is typical for a central bank. The Treaty on European Union unequivocally states, "The primary objective of the ESCB shall be to maintain price stability." Its mission statement has none of the ambiguous terms and controversial language found in the statutes of many other central banks, including those of the U.S. Federal Reserve. Although the ESCB certainly does have other responsibilities, *price stability,* or inflation control, is the institution's most important objective.

But why is price stability so holy? Why must inflation be so religiously controlled?

The answer is clear: Inflation is perhaps the greatest persistent threat to economic stability and growth. It is defined as a continuous rise in a country's general price level, and it reduces the value (i.e., buying power) of every note and coin in circulation in an economy. A more practical definition of inflation is "too much money chasing after too few goods." When demand for goods and services in an economy exceeds that which can be efficiently produced with its current stock of labor, capital, and technology (i.e., there is an economic boom), the economy overheats and businesses are forced to raise prices in order to suppress demand. When this occurs throughout an economy, it exacts a terrible toll on the delicate balance of production, consumption, and investment. In postwar inflationary Germany, men and women stood in endlessly long lines to purchase basic produce with carts of Hitler's reichsmarks. Though reichsmarks were legal tender at the time, inflation made them worth almost less than the paper they were printed on.

Yet inflation is dangerous even in less extreme instances. Indeed, its negative economic effects are as serious as they are numerous:

- It confuses customers. In the face of quickly rising prices, people have a difficult time establishing how much purchasing power their salaries actually offer. Consumer confidence dwindles, sending shock waves through the business world.

- It sends mixed signals to investors of all kinds. Imagine trying to make a $100 million corporate investment decision when your estimated equipment and real estate costs change monthly.

- It forces businesses and governments to constantly update and change prices. This consumes time, money, and energy that could be put to better use elsewhere.

- It increases the effective tax rate on capital, because assets are taxed on their quoted (or nominal) values. If your property's "real value" is only $100, but inflation has suddenly forced the price up to $150, you are taxed on the latter value, not the former. Regardless of whether inflation has forced your wages up as well, the effective tax rate on your property increases.

- Inflation has an important signaling effect. Unsteady prices send signals to markets worldwide that a country's government is neither steady nor well managed. This in turn leads to uncertainty, capital flight, higher borrowing costs, and economic stagnation.

As with all central banks, the principal means by which the ECB controls inflation is by influencing the level of inter-bank interest rates. Higher interest rates raise the cost of borrowing and thus decrease consumption. They also make saving look more attractive, spurring many businesses and consumers to hold onto their money rather than spend it. Accordingly, higher interest rates decrease aggregate demand for goods and services. This in turn suppresses economic growth and reduces inflation. Conversely, lower interest rates increase aggregate demand and spur economic growth. This basic process is the cornerstone of any industrialized economy.

The most important thing to remember about the ECB is that it is responsible for price stability *throughout the single-currency zone.* In effect, there is now one central bank where there were once eleven.

The question then arises: What does "price stability" mean in an economic zone that covers almost 1 million square miles? The answer is problematic because inflation may appear in some European countries even while it recedes in others. What happens if Portugal booms while Spain stagnates? Or if the Mediterranean nations go into recession while their northern counterparts witness an economic resurgence that drives prices upward? Such divergences are hardly nonsensical. The business cycle, as economists know it, pervades the industrialized world and impacts countries neither identically nor simultaneously. In 1997, for example, Ireland grew by over 10 percent, while Germany grew by barely 2.5 percent. Consequently, in 1998, Irish real estate and producer prices began to inflate, a sure sign that it was time to raise interest rates to cool down the economy.

Yet when Ireland handed over its monetary policy reins to the European Central Bank, the opposite occurred. The ECB *lowered* Irish interest rates to roughly the level prevailing in Germany and France at the time. The next few years are now likely to see a damaging inflationary trend in Ireland, because its interest rates are low compared to its rate of economic growth.

So why did the ECB lower Irish interest rates when higher interest rates were required? The short answer is easy: The ECB set a single interest rate for all of Euroland, not just for Ireland, and the rate it chose was simply less than that prevailing in Ireland in the period preceding the euro. But that leads to the larger question: Why didn't the ECB choose a Euroland interest rate appropriate to Ireland's situation?

The interest rate mismatch in Ireland occurred because the ECB examines a wide range of consumer and producer price indexes and money supply measures, any one of which plays only a very small role in determining general European price stability. When price levels in 10 of the 11 Euroland nations remain stable while those in the other skyrocket, the average Euroland price level doesn't change very much. That is exactly why the Treaty on European Union created the *convergence criteria* as EMU's entry requirement. The drafters of the Treaty "quite deliberately included in the Treaty the famous convergence criteria in order to ensure that countries wanting to participate in the euro area should have to demonstrate, before they were allowed to join, at least a minimum degree of sustainable convergence precisely in order to reduce the risk of divergent national monetary policy needs once the single currency is introduced."[34] Now that the euro is actually here, however, the convergence criteria offer little comfort. Persistent signs of divergence will pose a great challenge to the ECB for many years to come.

The ECB does have other responsibilities besides defending the general price level, though they are all secondary. First, it is required to support the general economic policies of the EU, provided that this task does not interfere with its duty to maintain price stability. This means that the ECB will periodically intervene in foreign exchange markets, a role discussed in question 25. Second, the ECB is responsible for ensuring the effectiveness of payment settlement throughout Euroland. If electronic transfers between banks, financial institutions, firms, and individuals do not run smoothly and securely, the euro's integrity is comprised. The management of payment settlement consists primarily of overseeing Europe's computerized cross-border payment system known as the Trans-European Auto-mated Real-time Gross settlement Express Transfer system (TARGET). Finally, the ECB is charged with protecting the financial reserves (e.g., foreign currency, securities, gold) of its member states.

18. How independent is the ECB, and why is this important?

The European Central Bank is considered the most independent central bank ever created. *Independent* in this context simply means "immune from the interests and influence of governments." This means that short-term political gain is unlikely to play a major role in the formulation of monetary policy in the new Europe.

The independence question is critically important because the same force that spurs consumer optimism and short-term economic growth (wonderful things for elected politicians) also unleashes inflation; and that force is a large supply of money. Hence, politicians seeking popular support and reelection often pressure monetary authorities into maintaining a relatively large money supply, even at the risk of inducing long-term inflation. But the longer-term effect of inflation is undeniably negative (see previous question). Quite naturally, then, anyone with a vested interest in European economic stability is now wondering whether the ECB will be sufficiently independent to ensure a vigorous fight against political interests.

So far, the news has been good, because no central bank is more independent than the ECB. This follows from several important facts. First and foremost, the ECB's defining statutes are unequivocal, stating, "neither the ECB, nor a national central bank, nor any member of their decision-making bodies shall seek or take instructions from Community institutions or bodies, from any Government of a Member State or from any other body." In many countries, however, heavy political influence on the central bank is not unusual. Even the highly independent U.S. Federal Reserve is more politicized than its new European counterpart. As Henry Kissinger writes, "The Federal Reserve Bank was established after America had created its political institutions. Legally independent, a thoughtful Fed chairman nevertheless is in close touch with the Treasury Department, aware of the views of the president and sensitive to congressional currents. He does not have to follow their preferences, but he would be reckless to ignore them consistently. By contrast, the ECB is free-standing without a political reference point."[35] The ECB is truly a supranational organization.

Second, the ECB is strictly prohibited from lending money to any EU government. This ensures that the central bank is detached from the financial interests of elected politicians. Hence, it is impossible for the ECB to become a money machine that prints euros to finance excessive national spending.

Third, the ECB is not subject to any unusual or inhibiting restrictions by national governments. That is, the EU is constitutionally required to accept ECB policies without any form of temporary meddling or interference. Even the world's most independent central bank before the euro, the German Bundesbank, was threatened by temporary two-week policy vetoes by the German government. No such veto exists against the ECB.

Fourth, the statutes that define ECB independence would be extremely difficult to repeal. Indeed, they could only be altered with a revision of the Treaty on European Union itself, an act that would require a *consensus* among the 15 member nations of the EU. This necessarily means that it would be at least as difficult to alter ECB independence as it was in the most strict such country before the euro. A single vote in opposition would foil any attempt. Hence, the U.S. Congress could revoke the Federal Reserve's independence more easily than the EU could threaten that of the ECB.

It would be unfair to conclude this question, however, without mentioning that whispers of political interference already haunt the corridors of European monetary policy. A highly publicized 1997–1998 controversy over the ECB's presidency has already cast some doubt on the central bank's constitutional independence. France forwarded its own candidate, Jean-Claude Trichet, while a large German-led majority insisted on Wim Duisenberg. The battle ultimately ended in an ugly compromise to informally split the eight-year presidential term in two, giving each candidate a four-year stint. In short, political compromise has already shaped the ECB's operation.

Critics of the euro claim that the theory of ECB independence is great, but that reality could easily be less than ideal. The minimum term of office for Governing Council members is only five years, and the hope of reappointment may encourage those seated to listen too intently to their governments' wishes. Governments do certainly have their own opinions on how monetary policy in Euroland should unfold. France is unquestionably the biggest counterweight in this regard. President Jacques Chirac hopes "to provide orientations" and "to clearly stake out the limits of [the ECB's] activities,"[36] and he has already taken specific actions to do so by creating a special "Euro-11" committee to periodically debate the general direction of European economic and monetary affairs. Though the Euro-11 committee has absolutely no voting or administrative powers, it represents a symbolic chink in the ECB's armor of independence. Only time will tell whether the ECB acts in a consistently independent fashion.

19. How is the ECB organized, and who's in charge of monetary policy?

The president of the European Central Bank is Willem ("Wim") F. Duisenberg, former president of the European Monetary Institute and the Central Bank of the Netherlands. Duisenberg is Europe's counterpart to Alan Greenspan and thus one of the most important leaders of the industrialized world. He will most likely serve as ECB president for four years, from 1999 to 2003, before retiring and being succeeded by the Frenchman Jean-Claude Trichet.

The management and administration of the ESCB is overseen by the ECB executive board. It consists of six members:

- Wim Duisenberg, president of the ECB, former head of the Central Bank of the Netherlands

- Christian Noyer, vice president of the ECB, former head of the French Ministry for Economic Affairs, Finance and Industry

- Otmar Issing, former chief economist of the German Bundesbank

- Tommaso Padoa-Schioppa, former deputy director general of the Bank of Italy

- Eugenio Domingo Solans, former executive board member of the Bank of Spain

- Sirkka Hämäläinen, former governor of the Bank of Finland

The board operates on a one-person, one-vote majority basis, with the tie-breaking vote belonging to Duisenberg.

The key monetary policy decision-making body of the ESCB is the ECB Governing Council. The Governing Council consists of the six members of the Executive Board plus the heads of the 11 national central banks. The Council meets at least 10 times a year to discuss European economic stability and to formulate monetary policy; it currently meets every other Thursday. The Council's announcements are highly anticipated by global financial markets. Periodically, the Governing Council also convenes in special sessions that include the heads of the four nonparticipating EU central banks. This "General Council," however, holds no decision-making authority.

20. What is the monetary policy strategy of the ECB?

The pursuit of European price stability is a noble but terribly unspecific goal. Hence, the first task of any newly founded central bank is to determine the method with which monetary policy is to be conducted. It is not enough to say that inflation is detrimental. Central bankers must also have a specific set of economic strategies that guide their efforts.

Generally speaking, the advanced industrialized world is characterized by two types of strategies: inflation targeting and money supply targeting. The ECB currently employs a combination of both.

Money supply targeting refers to the technique with which central banking officials predict future inflationary pressures by tracking the current amount of "money" in an economy. *Money* includes more than just notes and coins in people's pockets. In fact, *money supply* is usually used synonymously with technical terms like *M1, M2,* and *M3.* M3, the largest of these three measures, is roughly equal to the total amount of cash people have on hand, plus the total value of checking accounts, savings accounts, loan accounts, and similar short-term bank accounts in an economy at a given time. Put simply, measures like M3 correspond to the total amount of money in an economy that is immediately available to purchase goods and services. Your 10-year savings bond, pension balance, and rare coin collection aren't included, because they can't be immediately liquidated. But your checking balance and savings account are important components of the money supply.

Central bankers believe that the money supply is an excellent leading indicator of inflation. Why? Because inflation is best thought of as "too much money chasing after too few goods," and you can't buy goods without money. By tracking the total amount of cash, checking account balances, credit card limits, and similar balances, central banks can get a good idea of whether consumption is likely to go up or down in the near future. If the money supply appears large relative to the money supply target that the ECB sets each year, the ECB raises interest rates to discourage borrowing and spending.

But things get a little more complicated. Unfortunately, the newly created ECB does not have an extensive history, and thus has not yet established a good mathematical relationship between the money supply and the rate of inflation in Europe. Moreover, many economists think the advent of EMU itself will disrupt traditional money supply assumptions because the conversion process forces people to change their "money-holding habits" in a short period of time. As a result, the ECB also employs direct inflation targeting, a technique used in countries such as Britain and Sweden (and in Finland and Spain before EMU). In practice, this means that in addition to the money supply, the ECB also closely examines the price level itself and does whatever is necessary to keep it within predesignated bounds, regardless of what money supply measures like M3 suggest.

The ECB defines a change in the price level as a year-on-year increase in the harmonized index of consumer prices (HICP), the official Europen cost-of-living index. Specifically, the ECB announced that it will take whatever monetary policy actions are necessary to ensure that the HICP inflation rate remains in the range of 2 per cent or less.

Keeping track of the euro money supply and Euroland inflation level doesn't always yield easy answers. Due to the size, complexity, and diversity of the European Union, the ECB governing board examines a range of other indicators, from credit growth and consumer optimism in Holland to producer prices and industrial output levels in Italy. The ECB studies this mishmash of "other factors" so that it can conduct a "broadly based assessment of the outlook for price developments and the risks to price stability." Thus, the ECB's monetary policy strategy is actually a flexible one, with three supporting pillars: (1) control of the euro money supply, (2) direct monitoring of Euroland inflation rates, (3) examination of other price-related indicators.

21. How does the ECB conduct monetary policy?

When the ECB governing board decides that the supply of euros is growing too quickly or too slowly or that there are incipient signs of inflation, it uses a variety of monetary policy instruments to steer the economy in a new direction. By and large, these instruments are based on free-market operations, meaning that the ECB employs no artificial price caps, or tariffs in the course of its work. It simply sees itself as one extremely important player in the financial marketplace, with a particular investment goal: to control the overall money supply.

Because banks and other lending institutions are the main arteries of the business world, monetary policy begins on the banking balance sheet. Banks accept deposits from their customers (usually in the form of checking and savings accounts) and grant credit to (and therefore make investments in) a wide variety of endeavors. The difference between the interest rates they pay to their depositors and what they earn from their investments is profit.

Of course, banks don't lend out every euro they receive in deposits. They have to keep a small percentage of hard cash on hand to handle daily withdrawals, that is, to meet the liquidity needs of their depositors. Banks not only want to hold such cash reserves, the ECB also requires them to do so. In fact, the *minimum reserve requirement* is the ECB's most basic monetary policy tool, because it requires banks to deposit a certain amount of money in ECB accounts, where it can't be touched. This money is called, appropriately, *central bank money.* In a very direct fashion, then, the minimum reserve requirement keeps a certain amount of money out of circulation and thus reduces the euro money supply. The ECB pays banks a small amount of interest on the minimum reserves held in its vaults, but central bank money cannot be lent under any circumstances.

Though the minimum reserve requirement is an important monetary policy instrument, it plays a secondary role in daily ECB operations. The ECB's main means of influencing the European monetary supply involves *short-term refinancing operations.*

To understand how these operations work, imagine that you are the president of a European bank and that the ECB's minimum reserve requirement is 10 percent. Your depositors have left you with €1 million this month. Of that €1 million, you invest €500,000 in commercial loans to various businesses in your country and €400,000 in safe, interest-bearing government bonds. You keep the remaining €100,000 (10 percent of your deposits) at the ECB, pursuant to the minimum reserve requirement.

But suddenly things change. After all, banks are very busy places. Your depositors make some large commercial purchases, and they would like to withdraw €80,000 from their accounts to pay for them. Where do you get the money? The only cash you actually have is sitting at the ECB. Your only choice is to transfer €80,000 from your ECB account to your depositors.

Suddenly, you no longer meet the ECB's minimum reserve requirement. You have €920,000 in remaining deposits, but only €20,000 in your ECB account, well below the 10 percent minimum reserve requirement. In order to obey the banking laws, you need some money. And you need it fast.

You solve the problem by accepting a loan from the ECB. The ECB does this by buying some of the high-quality government bonds you own, on the strict condition that you buy them back two weeks later. This agreement gives you hard cash immediately (i.e., a temporary liquidity boost). The transaction you entered into with the ECB is called a *reverse repurchase agreement,* or repo. When the ECB buys, say, €72,000 of the €400,000 in government bonds you hold, it pays you by transferring money directly into your ECB account. Suddenly your central bank account holds €92,000 (€20,000 plus €72,000), or 10 percent of the €920,000 you have in deposits. You meet the minimum reserve requirement. Two weeks down the road you buy back the government bonds from the ECB for a price higher than that for which you sold them, say, €75,000. In essence, the repo transaction functioned as a loan. The ECB gave you the money you needed (€72,000), and you repaid it, with a little bit of *interest,* two weeks later (€75,000).

Now you have discovered something wonderful: You can temporarily break your minimum reserve requirement and still make a lot of money, because the ECB will refinance your minimum reserve shortfall for a small charge. Though the ECB charged you for your shortfall, you were able to lend more money to a commercial venture that earned 9 to 10 percent.

But how do all of these purchases and repurchases function as a monetary policy instrument?

Now that you know how a repo works, the answer is relatively straightforward: Repurchase transactions have an interest charge, and interest charges increase the overall cost of bank refinancing. The higher the cost of refinancing (i.e., obtaining money from one party in order to lend it to someone else), the fewer loans European banks are willing to offer. High repo interest rates raise the cost of lending money that is supposed to be held as a minimum reserve, which in turn makes many potential investments (e.g., loans) look less enticing to banks than they otherwise would. Alternatively, when the interest rate on ECB repurchase transactions is low, banks don't mind dipping below their minimum reserve requirements and lending a little extra. They know they can always refinance the loans by borrowing from the ECB at a low rate.

The crux of all this is that the fewer loans banks grant, the lower is the money supply. The money supply, if you remember, is the total amount of money in an economy that is available to purchase goods and services in the near future. When banks cut back on their lending practices, people and businesses have less spending money.

Though this is the basic transmission mechanism between higher interest rates on repurchase transactions and the money supply, it is important to know that the preceding scenario is greatly oversimplified. In fact, some important details about how ECB refinancing actually works follow:

- The EU is home to over 10,000 credit institutions of various kinds, each of which faces the basic refinancing challenge just outlined and contributes to the total amount of credit granted in the single-currency zone. Hence, monetary policy starts with the ECB but is transmitted through many financial institutions across the continent.

- Financial institutions do not always go to the ECB to borrow for their liquidity requirements; they often borrow from each other. Interbank lending is more common than central bank lending, and the ECB lends only when the banking system as a whole has a liquidity shortfall.

- The minimum reserve requirement is much lower than 10 percent. The ECB can change the minimum reserve requirement at any time, but it has announced that its target range will be between 1.5 and 2.5 percent of relevant bank liabilities.*

- Banks do not have to meet the minimum reserve requirement every day of the week. Rather, the ECB looks at monthly averages, and therefore banks do not have to run to the ECB after every unexpected withdrawal. As profit seekers, banks use intuition and experience to walk a fine line between meeting the minimum reserve requirement and falling short of it. Reserves held with the ECB also pay a small amount of interest, currently equivalent to the interest rate on its two-week repurchase transactions.

- If a bank decides it is lending too liberally, it can't just cancel loans that are too expensive to refinance. As a result, ECB interest rate changes can take many months to impact the actual lending behavior of banks. In fact, statistical evidence shows that changes in repurchase interest rates can take up to 18 months to impact consumption and investment levels.

---

* The liabilities used in this calculation are known as a bank's *reserve base*. The reserve base consists of overnight deposits, deposits with a maturity of up to two years, debt securities issued, debt securities with maturity of up to two years, and money market paper.

- The ECB conducts its refinancing activities through the 11 national central banks that make up the ESCB; it does not engage in repurchase transactions directly. The other 11 members of the ESCB work on behalf of the ECB to implement monetary supply goals.

- The ECB actually has two main types of refinancing operations. Once a week (currently on Tuesdays), it engages in short-term repurchase transactions with a two-week buyback deadline. These are known as its *main refinancing operations.* Once a month (currently on a Wednesday) the ECB offers *long-term refinancing,* that is, repurchase agreements with a three-month buyback deadline.

- All ESCB repurchase transactions are done on an open-market basis. The ESCB first decides how much (or how little) money it wants to grant to the banking system as a whole in order to meet its own goal for money supply growth. It then enters into repurchase agreements through standard tenders, meaning that European financial institutions submit bids to their national central banks stating the amount of money they need and interest rate they are willing to pay for it. The central banks then accept the free-market bids on an ordered best-offer basis. Banks bid only as much as they feel they can economically put to good use.

Repurchase rates are not the only interest rates that the ECB manipulates to regulate the money supply. Though they are less important in the European monetary policy picture, several "standing facilities" are also offered to financial institutions. The first, known as the *marginal lending facility,* is a sort of "emergency" loan that the ECB offers to any bank needing overnight liquidity. If one bank owes money to another but does not have the liquidity to pay the bill, or if it needs to take emergency action to meet its (monthly average) minimum reserve requirement, it can withdraw an unlimited amount of money as an outright overnight loan, no repurchases involved.* Because the marginal lending facility is available only for extremely short-term purposes, it acts as a sort of ceiling on interbank interest rates. No bank would pay 4 percent (annualized) interest to borrow money from another bank if it could pay 3.5 percent interest on a simple emergency loan from the ECB. Consequently, the ECB repo interest rate is almost always less than that offered by the marginal lending facility.

The second ECB standing facility is a short-term *deposit facility*. The opposite of a lending facility, this account allows banks to deposit on request an unrestricted amount of money at the ECB overnight in the event that they find themselves with more liquidity than they need. The ECB pays a small rate of interest on these deposits and serves as a last-resort place for banks to invest money when no other short-term options are available. Because any given bank would gladly lend to the ECB rather than to another bank at any given interest rate, the interest rate that the ECB pays on its overnight deposit facility is considered the floor rate for interbank lending. After all, why earn 0.5 percent by lending to another commercial bank when you can earn 1.0 percent lending to the ECB?

It is worth pointing out that the ECB's basic monetary policy instruments are similar to those used in Euroland before EMU and especially similar to those employed by the German Bundesbank. Repurchase transactions, the bread and butter of European monetary policy, were used in most of the 11 con-

---

* The withdrawal amount is technically limited to the value of a bank's collateral, but this is
  seldom a problem.

stituent national central banks long before 1999 and thus were a logical starting point when the ECB was created.

22. Who determines exchange rate policy for the euro zone?

The ECB, like all central banks, also plays an important role in foreign exchange markets. There are two main reasons for this. The first, not surprisingly, is that euro exchange rates impact European *price stability.* If the euro rapidly depreciates against the U.S. dollar, European goods suddenly become cheaper to Americans. The quite "sudden" increase in demand that results can ultimately heat up European economies, as they rush to fill booming export orders. This in turn can result in a rise in the general European price level, particularly because exports compose such an enormous portion of European GDP (see Chapter 2, Figure 2-2).

The second main reason for ECB involvement in euro exchange markets is that the ECB also endeavors to "support the general economic policies in the Community," insofar as its primary goal of price stability isn't threatened. In this regard, it is well known that exchange rates are a crucial determinant of industrial competitiveness. If they are volatile, economic growth begins to erode (see question 25). Equally important, euro exchange rates directly affect the price of goods and services sold abroad, as well as the cost of imports to Euroland. If the euro climbs, many European industries become less competitive and can even be priced out of their markets.

In fact, the euro's architects consider exchange rate stability and competitiveness issues to be so important that they involve parties other than the ECB in the exchange rate policy process. The most important of these is the EU Council of economics and finance ministers, commonly referred to as ECOFIN. ECOFIN is essentially the official outlet through which individual EU nations influence European economic policies. When ECOFIN meets, it discusses the broad goals of euro exchange rate policy and submits them to the European Central Bank. ECOFIN may decide, for instance, that the euro should be permitted to trade only in certain predefined bands against eastern European currencies such as the Polish zloty or Slovenian tolar. ECOFIN decisions are based on weighted majority vote, though only the 11 current participants vote on euro-related issues.

ECOFIN may determine general euro exchange rate regimes, but it is absolutely prohibited from making specific short-term intervention decisions. Only the ESCB intervenes directly in foreign exchange markets. It may try to alter the exchange rate value of a euro that it views as too high or too low by selling or buying large quantities of currency using the pool of assets donated by the national central banks when the ECB was created. But it does so without the direction of any external parties.

It merits mention that Europe does not have a single central government borrower like the U.S. Federal Treasury that is capable of influencing exchange rates. U.S. Treasury Secretary Robert Rubin can "talk the dollar up or down," when he sees fit, which in itself can be an important exchange rate tool. Government borrowing in the EU, however, is performed by each of the 11 national governments individually. Hence, the EU is left with a relatively bureaucratic ECOFIN committee that can issue only general suggestions and policies regarding exchange rates.

Chapter Summary

- The European Central Bank (ECB) is the highest monetary authority in the euro zone. Analogous to the

U.S. Federal Reserve, the Bank of Japan, or the German Bundesbank, the ECB is the issuer and constitutional guardian of the euro. In this capacity, it is the single most important determinant of the euro's ultimate stability and success.

- Although the ESCB does have other responsibilities, *price stability,* or inflation control, is the institution's single most important objective. Inflation confuses consumers, sends mixed signals to investors, forces businesses to constantly update prices, and increases the effective tax rate on capital.

- The European Central Bank is considered the most independent central bank ever created. It is guided by an unequivocal mission statement and is unattached to any single European government, which reduces the likelihood of political meddling in monetary affairs. The next few years, however, will offer the true test of the ECB's independence.

- The president of the European Central Bank is Willem ("Wim") F. Duisenberg, former president of the European Monetary Institute and the Central Bank of the Netherlands. The key decision-making body of the ECB is the Governing Council, whose membership includes Wim Duisenberg and the heads of the 11 national central banks.

- The ECB's monetary policy strategy is a flexible one, with three supporting pillars: (1) control of the euro money supply, (2) direct monitoring of Euroland inflation rates, and (3) examination of other price-related indicators. Using these techniques, the board sets the key interest rates that condition the pace of

European economic growth. Accordingly, short-term interest rates are now the same throughout Euroland.

- The ECB uses a handful of specific monetary policy instruments to control the euro money supply. They consist of (1) a minimum reserve requirement, (2) short-term repurchase transactions, (3) a marginal lending facility, and (4) a short-term deposit facility. Of these, repurchase transactions carried out through the 11 subordinate banks of the ESCB are the most important.

- Euro exchange rate changes not only impact price stability, but also affect general economic policies. As a result, the ECB works in conjunction with the EU Council of economics and finance ministers (ECOFIN) to establish Euroland's exchange rate policies. ECOFIN determines general euro exchange rate regimes (e.g., exchange rate agreements with non-EU countries), but is absolutely prohibited from making specific market interventions and from endangering price stability.

4
CHAPTER

The Euro's Effects on Business Environments Worldwide

The first three chapters of this book present the evolution, meaning, timing, and intricacies of Economic and Monetary Union, thereby describing the foundation upon which the new trans-European economy is built. By virtue of studying this foundation, you're now familiar with some of the euro's most important characteristics: its direct and indirect benefits, its costs and risks, the convergence criteria, the Stability & Growth Pact, the ECB, its Governing Council, and the banking transactions that shape European business cycles.

Nonetheless, some crucial questions concerning the euro's effects on worldwide business environments remain unanswered. Though the tools required to understand the importance and operation of monetary union have been introduced, it is time to consider their combined effects. What determines the euro's strength and stability, and what impact does this have on business environments? What role does the new currency play in European competitiveness and employment issues? How does the advent of monetary union affect stock and bond markets? What basic assumptions about the growth prospects and competitive dynamics of world business environments can no longer be taken for granted? The following pages address these and related topics.

23. How does a strong or weak euro affect the business world, and what specific factors determine the euro's strength?

Euro exchange rates set the tone for trade relations with Euroland, and businesses and investors worldwide are anxious to know whether the euro will be stronger or weaker than the national currencies that preceded it. When the euro is weak (meaning it trades at low levels against foreign currencies like the U.S. dollar), consumers pay lower prices for products imported from the euro zone. Non-European producers can even be priced out of their own markets amidst a deluge of cheap Euroland imports. When the euro is *too* weak, it sparks Euroland inflation and makes foreign borrowing by European firms and governments extremely expensive, thus destabilizing business environments. Alternatively, if the euro is strong, the export industries so crucial to European economic growth suffer, because non-Euroland countries have to pay more to buy euro-denominated products. Simultaneously, Euroland imports increase, galvanizing production in the region's main trading partners.

Like all currencies, the euro strengthens and weakens over time. The U.S. dollar fell against the Japanese yen for most of the past 30 years before reversing course in 1995. Between 1985 and 1998, one U.S. dollar bought as many as 3.3 German marks and as few as 1.4. Such shifts are anything but accidental. Above all else, currency strength is a function of supply and demand. Simply put, currencies rise when investors want to put their money into investments denominated in those currencies. Demand for investments, in turn, is directly related to confidence in the issuers. Is there a risk that the French government could default on the billions of dollars of government bonds it issues every year? Do Finnish corporations offer solid long-term earnings prospects? Global financial markets put forth such questions incessantly, and the answers play a crucial role in determining demand for euros.

So, what determines whether investors are getting the answers they want to hear concerning the prospects of Euroland investments? Following is a list of the five factors that determine overall investment demand, as well as the current prognoses for Euroland.

General political, economic, and fiscal stability. Stable economic environments are home to excellent investments.

When financial markets fear that budgetary problems, political discord, or social unrest are beginning to endanger monetary union, they shun investments in the single-currency zone. Indeed, every piece of instability-signaling information that enters the marketplace chips away at quoted euro values. Particularly troublesome to Euroland in this regard is its high level of unemployment (19 percent in Spain, 13 percent in Finland, 12 percent in Italy, and over 11 percent in Euroland as a whole) and the political uncertainty surrounding the entire single-currency project. Despite these risks, long-term interest rate analysis reveals that markets currently believe in the long-term viability and success of monetary union, a fact which suggests that the euro will be strong.

An important part of the general economic stability of Euroland is the ability of EU governments to "balance their books." Euro enthusiasts argue that the new currency will be strong, because the Stability & Growth Pact has already done much to improve the fiscal profile (i.e., spending habits) of EU governments. Under the pact, annual budget deficits are formally restricted to less than 3.0 percent of GDP (see question 5), a figure better than that prevailing, for instance, in the United States over a good part of the past two decades. Nonetheless, the Stability Pact is subject to significant exceptions and qualifications, and there is a risk that countries that have been fiscally profligate in the past may return to the days of large government budget deficits. For the time being, however, fiscal prognoses for the euro area are generally healthy, suggesting that the euro will be strong.

External trade position. Another critical determinant of economic stability, and thus of the euro's strength, relates to Euroland's external trade position. Put simply, when a country imports more than it exports, it runs a deficit in its *current account.* It consumes more than it produces, and it has to borrow from abroad to make up the difference. Financial markets view current account deficits as signs of long-term instability, just as stock market analysts view highly leveraged corporations as riskier than their low-debt counterparts. All other things held equal, countries with current account surpluses have strong currencies, and countries with current account deficits have weak ones.

At the moment it appears that Euroland's external trade position bodes well for a strong euro. Euroland as a whole is expected to have a current account surplus of about 2.7 percent of GDP in 1999.[37] The United States, in contrast, has run current account deficits for the last 16 years, forcing it to borrow massively from foreign countries like Japan. Indeed, the U.S. current account deficit was a key contributor to the sharp fall of the dollar against the yen during the latter half of the 1980s. Accordingly, expect global financial markets to keep a careful eye on Euroland's current account.

Inflation expectations. No one wants to invest in a currency that is unlikely to hold its value. As a result, all other things held equal, the euro weakens when long-term Euroland inflation increases. The euro's architects claim that this tends toward a strong currency, because the ECB is the most independent central bank ever created. Imbued with a well-defined goal of price stability, prohibited from financing budget deficits, modeled after the famously independent Bundesbank, and unattached to any single nation, the ECB fights inflation with what some call unprecedented zeal. Of course, that is not to say that political influence is nonexistent or that the ECB's monetary instruments are always effective in steering business cycles. But whatever the outcome, expect announcements of inflation-related statistics to be hotly anticipated by euro exchange markets. Euroland inflation currently stands at a healthy 1.4 percent.

Interest rate expectations. High Euroland interest rates attract investors wanting high returns, which in turn generates demand for euro-denominated assets. Though investors carefully balance the opportunities presented by high interest rates against the economic instability (e.g., inflation) that usually causes them, interest rate hikes increase the value of the euro against other currencies. In fact, high Euroland interest rates will likely produce a strong euro even if they are caused by irresponsible EU budget deficits that bloat European consumption and bring short-term inflation. This is exactly what happened to the United States in the first half of the 1980s. Ronald Reagan's enormous budget deficits, driven by massive defense expenditures, drove the U.S. Federal Reserve to continually increase interest rates in order to control rising inflation. Because financial markets worldwide believed in the Fed's ability to ultimately succeed in its task, foreign investors poured their money into the high-return U.S. investments created by rate hikes.

When the euro arrived in January of 1999, short-term Euroland interest rates were relatively low, particularly because Germany and France, which account for over half of Euroland's GDP (see Figure 4-1), were growing modestly and had relatively low inflation. (Note that Figure 4-1*a* and *b* shows the same information in two different formats.) The remarkable convergence of long-term rates, to about 5 percent, shows that financial markets are convinced that a low-inflation, low-interest rate environment is here to stay. To date, market participants truly believe in the independence and determination of the ECB. As business cycles rise and fall, however, interest rate expectations will change with them.

Reserve currency status. The final major determinant of the euro's strength is also the most uncertain. It relates to the euro's potential to become a major international reserve currency. If the single-currency zone does indeed remain sound and

F I G U R E   4-1a

Euroland's 11 economies.

Country	Contribution to Euroland GDP (%)
Germany	33.5
France	22.0
Italy	18.2
Spain	8.5
Netherlands	5.8
Belgium	3.8
Austria	3.2
Finland	1.9
Portugal	1.6
Ireland	1.2
Luxembourg	0.2

Source: Eurostat.

stable, euro exchange rates will receive an extra boost by the
massive shift in demand that results from the use of the euro as
a long-term store of value worldwide (see question 11). Daily
euro trading volumes will increase dramatically, transaction
costs for the currency will fall, and the euro will strengthen. The
euro's potential to become a major international reserve currency is discussed in question 24.

24. Does the euro pose a serious challenge to the supremacy of the U.S. dollar?

The euro has already become a critically important international reserve currency, not least by virtue of the fact that all
previous Euroland currencies, regardless of where they were

Euroland's 11 economies. (*Continued*)

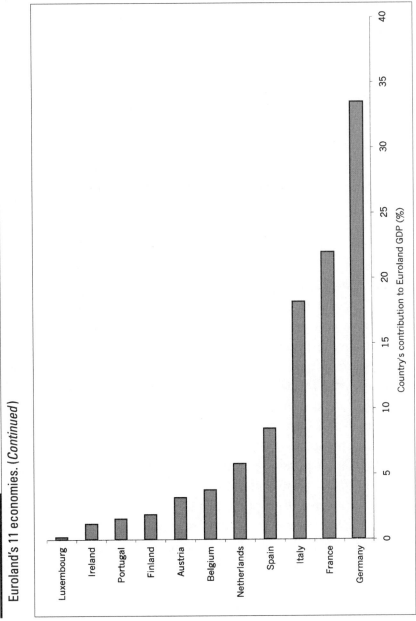

held, converted into euros on January 1, 1999. Not all curren-cies have reserve currency potential, but the euro is accepted as payment in a sufficiently broad area to make it a serious long-term challenger to the U.S. dollar. Euroland is now the world's second largest economy. It is also responsible for a larger pro-portion of world trade than is the United States.

Contrary to popular belief, however, the euro's ability to supersede the dollar as the world's premier reserve currency is dependent on far more than simple statistical comparisons. First, the emergence of a reserve currency depends not only on levels of international trade, but also on their respective growth rates. International trade as a percentage of the U.S. economy has been growing at a faster rate than similar trade figures for EU economies. Will this trend continue? Or is it coming to an end? Experts disagree.

Second, the overall size and depth of national capital mar-kets are no less important as determinants of reserve currency status than is trade in goods and services. As shown in Chapter 1, Figure 1-5, the combined size of U.S. stock and bond mar-kets is more than double that of Euroland. The United States is home, for example, to more than twice the number of publicly listed firms. Demand for U.S. financial assets spurs tremen-dous demand for the U.S. dollars needed to buy them. Will European corporations and investors, in the wake of the euro, finally develop an appetite for private sector stocks and bonds that will drive European capital markets to unprecedented sizes? Many observers think they will. Others believe that U.S. markets will reign for decades more.

Finally, long-term changes in the general fiscal and eco-nomic well-being of Europe compared to the United States directly impact worldwide portfolio diversification into euros. The U.S. economy's most bothersome feature to dollar inves-tors is its 16-year history of current account deficits. If this low-savings, high-consumption trend continues, investors worldwide are likely to see the euro as an increasingly attractive source of long-term value. The EU's most bothersome features to euro investors, on the other hand, are its structural rigidities and rampant unemployment problems. Though it is useful to look at the relative size of the U.S. and Euroland economies when examining the reserve currency picture, more pertinent information is found in the improvements that the two economies make to their basic structural problems.

The euro is already pulling some reserve currency "market share" away from the dollar, but do not expect any *major* change to the dollar's international status in the near future. As the president of Germany's Bundesbank points out, "Monetary history has shown that a key currency being superseded is ultimately due to an internal crisis in the country in question."[38] U.S. officials have echoed these remarks, because they firmly believe that a major shift out of dollars would occur only in the midst of domestic political or economic crisis. Just as the dollar was unable to unseat England's pound sterling as the world's premier reserve currency until a world war literally forced investors across the Atlantic, so is the euro unlikely to overtake the dollar any time soon.

25. How does a stable or unstable euro affect the business world, and what specific factors determine the euro's stability?

The euro's stability is at least as important as its strength, because a chronically unstable currency is the scourge of economic growth and investment. Unstable currencies rattle trade-dependent economies, destroy investments, and fracture business environments. When extreme exchange rate volatility persists, it not only slows consumption and investment, but also precipitates industrial chaos, social discontent, even political upheaval. An unstable euro would not only have damaging economic effects, it would also incur the wrath of voters in countries such as Germany, Belgium, the Netherlands, and Luxembourg—countries accustomed to a high level of external stability. The Asian currency crisis of the last several years, as evidenced in part by the experiences of countries like Indonesia, is testimony to the importance of currency stability. Indeed, the euro's general stability level between 1999 and 2005 will set the tone for economic and political union in Europe for decades to come.

Changes in euro stability are determined by many of the same factors that determine the euro's strength (see question 23). If the ECB succeeds in controlling inflation and maintains its reputation of strict independence, if general economic and fiscal stability and current account surpluses are here to stay, if the euro is viewed as a dependent long-term store of value, then financial markets have no reason to constantly reevaluate euro exchange rates. Against the current backdrop of political, economic, and monetary stability, exchange rate crises like those seen in East Asia, South America, or Russia in recent years are highly unlikely in Euroland. In this respect, experts do not expect Euroland's general stability level to change any time soon.

When it comes to short-term currency stability, however, long-term factors are far less important than daily changes in expectations of central bank behavior. Remember, changes in Euroland interest rates directly impact returns on euro-denominated investments. The more frequently interest rate expectations change, the more volatile the euro becomes. But how frequently are European interest rates expected to change? Will interest rate expectations themselves be relatively volatile, as they were in countries like Portugal, Italy, and Ireland before the euro?

The answer pivots on an important fact: The economic and monetary growth measures that are the basis for ECB interest rate decisions derive from a much larger economic area than those of any individual Euroland country. Regional demand changes and industry-specific inflationary bursts impact aggregate Euroland price indices much less significantly than they did national indices. Put simply, monetary policy is based on a more slowly changing economic area than a France, Italy, Ireland, or Belgium taken alone. Hence, interest rates in Euroland are expected to change less frequently than they did in many individual countries before the euro.

This fact, however, does not by any means ensure daily euro stability, because the ECB's exchange rate policies also have to be factored into the equation. Exchange rate movements can have a significant impact on inflationary pressures and can play a crucial role in determining the general economic competitiveness of export industries. In countries that trade heavily, even small exchange rate movements can make or break economic growth or substantially increase the threat of inflation. That is precisely why, prior to the euro, the central banks of such countries as Austria, Belgium, and Portugal meticulously monitored the value of their currencies against those of their major trading partners and reacted accordingly to keep exchange rates steady.

But euro exchange rates do not require the hands-on management and attention often seen in Europe before the euro. Why? Because the euro combines a group of small, open economies into one large, closed economy. Overnight, Euroland has been transformed from 11 distinct nations, in which exports accounted for an average of 44 percent of GDP, into a single economy in which exports account for a mere 10 percent of GDP. A shipment from Austria to the Netherlands is no longer considered an exchange rate–influencing export and is no longer prey to exchange rate fluctuations.

This has an important effect on exchange rate policy. As one prominent study puts it, "In a closed economy, monetary policy operates through interest rates and asset prices. . . . In an open economy, the exchange rate assumes paramount importance. . . . For these reasons, it is natural to expect the ECB will devote less attention to the exchange rate than has been the case with European central banks so far."[39] In other words, currency movements in a large, closed economy like Euroland aren't that bothersome to monetary policy. Imports and exports simply aren't as important to the general economic picture as they used to be, and exchange rate movements are thus less likely to spur inflation and endanger general industrial competitiveness in the region as a whole. Hence, the ECB is not inclined to intervene in foreign exchange markets very often.

Experts believe that this policy of "benign neglect" toward euro exchange rates will ultimately produce a relatively volatile euro. Whereas Belgium pegged its franc to the mark before EMU, religiously following Bundesbank interest rate changes and intervening in foreign exchange markets to maintain the franc's stability, the ECB is likely to let free markets reign. Banks, mutual funds, pension funds, and multinationals trade hundreds of millions of euros at a time, and speculators place massive bets on future euro values.

This, in turn, does anything but promote stability, and it will only worsen as the euro's role in international finance grows. Much of the U.S. dollar's volatility in the postwar period, for instance, is attributable to its use in a tremendous proportion of international transactions and its tendency to be the destination of investor flights from other currencies in times of crisis. Around 83 percent of two-way transactions in foreign exchange markets[40] and 48 percent of world export invoices[41] are based on the dollar. As a result, "foreign exchange markets can see great movements in the dollar, as much as 3% a month, month after month in the same direction."[42] As more foreign exchange traffic channels into euros, euro markets will behave similarly to U.S.-dollar markets.

The first few years of euro trading may be particularly volatile, because the euro project as a whole remains shrouded in uncertainty. The ECB is theoretically independent, but has no actual track record. Economic growth in several EU countries continues to diverge from the rest. Popular acceptance of a new currency has not been tested. As a result, daily expectations of the general economic health of Europe and the success of monetary union itself are particularly mercurial. Consequently, the freely floated euro is unlikely to trade in any narrow band.

26. How does the euro revolutionize European business markets in the long term?

Monetary union entails changes to European markets that go well beyond issues related to the strength and stability of the euro. In fact, any marketing study, investment recommendation, corporate strategy, or policy paper on the new European economy needs to take at least three general environmental trends into account. Though the euro's immediate economic effects (e.g., increased price transparency) were discussed in detail in question 10, it is worth taking a moment to consider some long-term market-oriented consequences.

Financial backdrop.   European markets aren't as diverse as they used to be. Short-term interest rates are the same throughout the euro zone, a feat achieved only because countries like Spain dropped rates from over 13 percent in 1992 to around 4 percent today. Just six years ago, long-term interest rates in the region ranged from about 5.5 percent in Germany to over 9 percent in Portugal. Today, the difference is about 0.5 percent. Moreover, thanks to the convergence criteria and the Stability & Growth Pact, Euroland fiscal profiles are also broadly similar, as the 11 national budget deficits are now uniformly under 3 percent. Because the credit risk and financial stability of a business can't be better than that of its host country, this transformation has done much to equalize European private-sector risk.

This general economic convergence is especially pronounced when considered against the backdrop of the common market. Among other things, the unrestricted flow of goods, services, capital, and labor was designed to promote prosperity and growth in the EU's "peripheral" economies, a term that generally refers to the lower-income areas of Greece, Ireland, Italy, Portugal, and Spain. These countries have indeed boomed in the midst of the common market, and they are currently growing at a tremendous pace. This is enhanced still further by the massive fiscal transfers designed to equalize living standards in the EU. Portugal, for example, receives over $11 million a day from EU transfer programs, money that has gone directly to bring its highway systems, telephones access, and other public works up to the standards of its northern neighbors. Ireland, Greece, Spain, and Italy are also net beneficiaries of the EU budget.

European expansion. The second major business trend that the euro catalyzes concerns the perception of Euroland as a single expansionary environment. Because the euro eliminates currency-related transaction costs and exchange rate risk, promotes cross-border competitive pricing, creates deep financial markets, and cements the idea of a single European market, firms are beginning to reorganize themselves as pan-European concerns. The economies of scale and efficiency gains promised by a customer base of almost 300 million people has already led to a stream of banking mergers. Insurance and other financial services mergers are likely to constitute the next wave, with major service and manufacturing merger waves to follow.

An important aspect of trans-European strategic expansion is that countries are better able to use their comparative advantages to attract investment from across the Continent. Experts expect, for instance, a substantial amount of manufacturing production to switch to the "periphery" economies, with their lower labor costs and comparatively inexpensive real estate. Similarly, the high-skill, service-sector prowess of German, French, Dutch, and Belgian multinationals is now a more formidable force in those countries' southern neighbors.

Policy harmonization. The third major market trend instituted by the euro involves the continued harmonization of market-related public policies. Most prominently, the new currency is likely to lead to long-term tax harmonization among the 11 participating nations. As Figure 4-2 shows, European tax rates vary considerably. Germany's sales tax is 16 percent, while France's is 20 percent and rising. The marginal corporate tax rate spread between neighboring Austria and Italy is almost 20 percent. (Note that Figure 4-2*a* and *b* shows the same information in two different formats.)

Experts believe that the ease of Euroland capital flight ushered in by the euro puts tremendous pressure on governments to compete for the lowest tax rates in order to attract high-skilled labor and corporate investments. Price transparency makes tax differences on goods and services clearer than ever. In fact, Luxembourg's low tax rates on bank deposits have already attracted billions of dollars of European capital

F I G U R E 4-2a

Euroland's taxman.

Country	Value-Added Tax Rate (%)	Marginal Corporate Tax Rate (%)
Denmark	25.0	34
Finland	22.0	28
Ireland	21.0	38
Belgium	21.0	40.2
France	20.0	36.7
Austria	20.0	34
Italy	19.0	53.2
The Netherlands	17.0	35
Portugal	17.0	36
Spain	16.0	35
Germany	16.0	48.4
Luxembourg	15.0	34.3

Source: *Die Woche, Europa Interview, DM Magazin*, European Commission.

flight. The unprecedented corporate tax subsidies that Ireland has dished out in recent years have attracted tremendous international investment, but have also incurred the wrath of EU bureaucrats from countries on the losing end of the bargain. Though national competitiveness pressure has always played a role in EU tax policy, a single trans-European currency ensures that intra-Euroland tax competition, and perhaps harmonization, will reach unseen heights in the next decade.

Despite the fact that all three of the euro's primary market effects deal with consolidation and harmonization, it is wise not to exaggerate these points. Euroland remains an extremely heterogeneous place, with 11 distinct governments, cultures,

Euroland's taxman. (*Continued*)

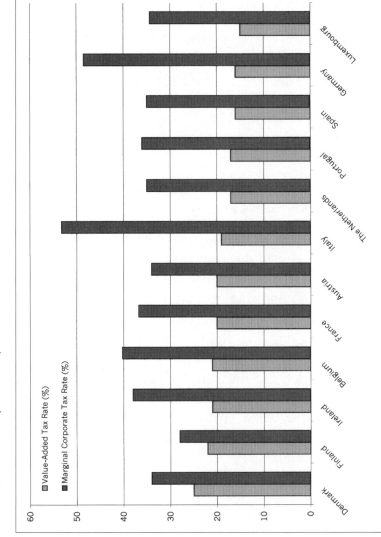

and official languages. In the short term, the euro does nothing to equalize the tremendous differences in productivity, industrial competitiveness, product quality, local tastes, and legal environments that have always characterized the European Union. Personal income, for instance, varies from 219 percent of the EU average in wealthy Hamburg to about 30 percent of the average in the rural Portuguese Azores. Equivalent U.S. figures vary only between 141 and 73 percent.[43]

27. Does the euro solve Europe's chronic unemployment and competitiveness problems?

As the president of the European Central Bank has stated, "The [European Union] does not have a good record in terms of job creation. Unemployment in most member states, though showing signs of stabilizing, remains high, and the situation in labor markets is forecast to remain highly unsatisfactory. A wide range of institutional rigidities account for the weak employment performance, and it will be a major challenge to tackle them in a decisive manner."[44] Indeed, average unemployment in the EU is over 11 percent (compared with 5.4 percent in the United States), almost twice what it was in 1979. According to another observer, "more new jobs were created in the U.S. in two months than in the EU over the past 10 years."[45]

Does the euro bring a solution to this painful problem?

In the short and medium term, the euro does little or nothing to ease Europe's acute unemployment situation, despite a glut of political claims to the contrary. The reason is that the euro does nothing to reform the fundamental problems that economists say create Europe's high levels of unemployment. It is extremely important to remember what the euro does and does not accomplish. The euro does not automatically introduce lower corporate taxes or simplify the complex tax laws that dominate European business environments. In fact, in 1996, taxes in the EU hit record levels as a percentage of GDP. The euro does not bring an end to overbearing business regulations, accelerate privatization, or curb corporate subsidies. It does nothing to reduce Europe's enormous welfare state transfers or to reduce its high manufacturing labor costs, which by 1998 were 12 percent higher than those in the United States.[46] It does not cure Europe's poor record in information technology. In short, the new currency does not bring fundamental structural change to European nations; it unifies existing systems.

In the long term, the euro's unemployment effects remain unclear. In fact, two powerful and conflicting interpretations have emerged on the subject. The first holds that the euro will ultimately be a boon to employment, because EMU's basic economic consequences are forcing European governments to implement the structural reforms that are needed to reduce long-term unemployment (see question 11). More generally, enthusiasts claim that the reduced transaction costs, low interest rates, and deep financial networks that the euro presents are leading Europe to a higher long-term growth trajectory. If the euro's core economic benefits do indeed push European economies into an era of higher economic growth, millions of new jobs will be created in the next decade alone.

The opposing school of thought argues that the euro's employment effects are no better in the long term than they are in the short term. Stated simply, euro pessimists argue that the new currency leaves participating nations helpless in the wake of economic shocks and that unemployment levels in economically divergent countries will reach unprecedented levels. Without independent interest rate adjustments, flexible labor markets, or fiscal transfers between European countries, the argument goes, the euro is destined to bring massive instability and stagnancy, with millions of job losses to follow (see question 13).

Whichever school is correct, the outcome will not be known for many years. But the ongoing employment controversy remains at the center of the new trans-European economy and underlines one of the euro's greatest ironies: It is totally unclear whether Europe's most sweeping economic policy change in the postwar period does anything to solve its most acute problem.

28. How does the euro affect business markets outside of Europe?

Most important, the euro establishes a whole new set of relationships between European firms and the prices of their goods and services in foreign markets. As discussed in question 23, the strength or weakness of the euro—as opposed to the mark or the lira—is now the critical variable in the trade equation.

Apart from this fundamental change, however, three principal long-term effects of the new currency are worth knowing. First, it is conceivable that the euro's emergence as a major international reserve currency may negatively impact the cost of borrowing for U.S. institutions, including governments and firms. In short, the appearance of a new alternative to dollar investments may decrease the demand for American securities. If dollar-denominated markets become smaller and less liquid, the cost of borrowing to U.S. issuers increases. This may be particularly troublesome to U.S. efforts to finance its $160 billion current account deficit (see question 23), but the effect may ultimately manifest itself in all American securities, from corporate bonds in Texas to high-tech IPOs on Wall Street. The next few decades will reveal exactly what role the euro is destined to play in international finance.

A second international effect is that economies with traditionally strong links to Europe, such as the promising markets of eastern Europe, North Africa, and the CFA French franc zone, are likely to start invoicing trade in euros. Much of this process is already under way, because the existing European currencies frequently used in these areas automatically convert into euros. The promise now exists, however, that the enormous size and liquidity of euro-based economies will exert an unprecedented influence in these regions, resulting in the conversion of these important economic blocs into euro trading zones long before the euro has a more general impact on worldwide U.S. dollar reserves.

Third, if the euro does, as its architects claim, enable European firms to substantially increase their size, strength, and capital-raising capacities, then those same firms are likely to use their newfound advantages as the lever of expansion into foreign markets. Just as U.S. firms have been able to use economies of scale in their domestic market as a springboard to international success, so may many international markets come under attack from previously unseen Euroland competitors. The financial institution, durable goods manufacturer, or consulting service that once felt restricted by the vagaries of European exchange rate risk may grow to the point where expansion into American, Asian, or Middle Eastern markets becomes a foregone conclusion.

29. What are the euro's principal effects on stock markets?

An important part of any business environment is the size, scope, and sophistication of its financial markets. And even in this realm, the euro hardly leaves a stone unturned.

For starters, the euro creates the second-largest stock market in the world. On a technical level, this transformation was

relatively straightforward: Publicly traded shares on Euroland's major exchanges converted to euros on the first trading
day of 1999. The recalculation of share values occurred automatically, because free markets determine share prices, and
market participants have been perfectly capable of applying the
official euro exchange rates to their own buy and sell orders.
The conversion of common stock par values on corporate balance sheets is a minor accounting change and did not (and generally will not) affect the new trading values.

Apart from the technical detail that major exchanges now
list shares in euros,* the advent of monetary union has serious
ramifications for European public and private equity markets.
Currently, the Euroland equity landscape remains fractured and
disparate, a legacy of the days of 11 national currencies and
their resulting transaction costs. Euroland's 28 stock exchanges
are indeed a hallmark of inefficiency and regionalism. The
United States, by comparison, supports a stock market capital-
ization of many times the size with a quarter the number of
exchanges. In Euroland, most trades occur within national borders, but in the United States and Japan, equity markets are
thoroughly national. Euroland households are also extremely
risk-averse, as evidenced in part by the fact that only about 5
percent of people in countries like Germany own any stock at
all. Europeans tend to like their bankers better than their stock-
brokers.

The euro, however, is widely expected to result in a general trend of expansion, consolidation, and sophistication that
will make European equity markets more competitive with

---

* Note that the conversion of stock values to euros on the first trading day of 1999 is a rare
  exception to the "no compulsion, no prohibition" rule discussed in question 2 because
  it forces investors to transact in euros immediately. In some countries (e.g., Germany),
  special laws were passed to make this exception permissible.

their American and Japanese counterparts. This view rests on several supporting pillars. First, common prices and the elimination of exchange rate risk are likely to spur Euroland investors—individuals and institutions alike—to jump into equity investments in other Euroland countries to an extent never previously seen. Put simply, it has never been easier and cheaper for Europeans to buy foreign securities. Second, enthusiasts argue that the euro's core economic advantages have propelled Euroland into a golden economic era of private-sector consolidation, low government spending, monetary stability, and high growth. In short, they argue that Europe is poised for a long-term economic boom and that investors will flood into stocks with newfound zeal as annual returns rise. Third, Euroland equity markets have in some ways been unnaturally constrained for decades, because market fragmentation along national borders ensured that financial innovations lacked the base of investors necessary to make them successful. Indeed, the initial emergence of REITS, complex derivatives, venture capital, and even mutual funds in the United States is at least partially attributable to the country's enormous and unfragmented market of potential investors.

The upshot of all this is that experts expect European equity markets to blossom in the next decade. Existing exchanges will consolidate as trading volumes grow and domestic investors begin to take a pan-European view. Financial innovation and low transaction costs may ease European households out of their long-held aversion to stock markets. Though it is highly debatable how long it will take for such transformations to occur, important foundations have already been laid. Stock exchanges across Euroland now list shares in a common currency. American investment banks are beginning a massive transfer of their IPO and equity analysis expertise to their European operations. Pan-European stock indices like the Dow Jones Euro Stoxx and the FTSE Euratop 300 have already captivated the attention of investors worldwide.

From an overseas perspective, the euro also institutes some noteworthy changes. Among other things, U.S. investors and mutual funds are likely to increase portfolio diversification toward Europe for many of the same reasons that now galvanize European investors: the greater simplicity and transparency of pan-European investing. Moreover, the euro represents a major economic event, and if it's successful, it may provide excellent investment opportunities for people of all continents.

Other major effects of the euro on equity markets relate to exchange rate regimes. First, investors from New York to Beijing now bear a single type of exchange rate risk in most Euroland investment environments—that related to the strength or weakness of the euro. To the extent the euro is more or less stable than one of the preceding national currencies, monetary union totally overturns the investment inclinations of foreign institutions toward that country. If the euro is stable, Italy, Spain, and Portugal are particularly likely to benefit from their newfound "stable currency" reputations.

Second, regardless of the euro's stability, institutions worldwide are now inclined to approach European investing from a top-down rather than a bottom-up approach. Why? Before the euro, one of the major determinants of equity risk to a foreign investor was national currency risk. When the lira dropped in value, the returns on a stock listed on the Italian Stock Exchange, from the perspective of a U.S. investor, dropped with it. Accordingly, institutions tended to break up European investment targets along national lines, first selecting the level and type of country-specific exchange rate risk they were willing to accept and then selecting specific firms. The euro, however, makes this top-down approach obsolete, as Euroland now has a common level of exchange rate risk.

Like all of the euro's effects, it's important not to expect too much change too fast. To date, European equity markets remain highly fractured, with a range of tax environments, auditing procedures, accounting regulations, listing requirements, and client bases. Nonetheless, it is clear that the euro lays important groundwork for major changes to the European equity scene.

30. What are the euro's principal effects on bond markets?

If it is true that Europe's capital markets are experiencing greater change than at any time in the past century, then nowhere is the effect more pronounced than in Euroland's bond markets. The short-term changes alone are tremendous. Among other things, EU regulations now require all new government bonds to be issued in euros. The days of mark, markka, lira, and escudo public debt offerings are gone forever. Moreover, Euroland governments have relisted their immense outstanding pools of public bonds in euros, despite the fact that the EU's "no compulsion, no prohibition" rule doesn't strictly require them to do so (see question 2). Overnight, the euro has healed the currency-induced fractures of Euroland's 11 public debt markets, instantly creating a market of euro-denominated assets around the globe.

Bonds issued by parties other than central governments will convert into euros gradually between 1999 and 2002. This includes debt issues by state and local governments and corporations. By 2002, however, all payments of interest and principal on new or existing bonds denominated in one of the 11 national currencies must be paid in euro. On that date, at the latest, the total conversion of Euroland debt markets will be complete. It is important to point out, however, that the bulk of these public and private "redenominations" occur without official proceedings, bondholder meetings, or paperwork. EU law states that all national currencies became mere representations of the euro on January 1, 1999, at the irrevocably fixed exchange rates. As a result, bondholders are not in a position to make or lose value by virtue of the reexpression of a debt in euros, and no special proceedings are generally required.

Though Euroland bonds now feature a common currency, be careful not to confuse the sharp convergence among Euroland economies and the creation of a single unit of account with the elimination of national bond markets. The introduction of the euro does not change the fact that Europe has no central euro issuer like the U.S. Treasury that serves as the center of gravity for bond markets. Europe has no debt-issuing central government, and thus does not have a U.S. Treasury equivalent.

Consequently, though the ECB sets a single set of short-term interest rates throughout the euro zone, long-term rate differences among debt issuers persist. Such differences are, however, extremely narrow. As Figure 4-3 shows in both table and graph form, long-term interest rates in all EU countries converged remarkably in the period prior to EMU. Italy, for instance, despite its enormous federal debt, now pays only slightly more than Germany for its 10-year bonds, a spread larger than that found between U.S. states.[47]

But why did long-term interest rate convergence occur? The first reason, as previously discussed, is that the convergence criteria have brought about sharp *economic convergence* in the 11 euro participants (see question 5). From an investor's standpoint, the credit risks of various government issuers just aren't as disparate as they used to be. Second, a single currency strips away the exchange rate risk that used to wedge Euroland interest rates apart. Before the euro, Italian government bonds were considered far riskier than their German counterparts—and thus commanded a higher interest rate—partially because the lira was significantly more volatile than the mark. But now these various exchange rate premiums have vanished and have been replaced by a single type of currency risk for the whole region. As a result, differences in long-term Euroland interest rates are now primarily determined by credit and liquidity risks.

The euro also lays the foundation for significant long-term changes in Euroland's bond markets. Foremost, bond markets, like stock markets, are poised to become larger and more liquid than ever before. Before the euro, investors across the Continent, from heads of households to billion-dollar pension funds, were averse to—even legally prohibited from—making investments in other currencies for fear of exchange rate exposure.* But euro-denominated investments are now available to investors from Ireland to Austria, and this enormous investor base is expected to increase the liquidity of debt instruments of all types.

Second, the euro is expected to promote innovation and structural change. Most important, the European corporate debt market is expected to explode, because the larger base of potential investors for any given issue makes new instruments more feasible. Asset-backed securities also have become more realistic, because their hallmark feature—diversification across a wide range of independent investments—is now easier to achieve. Additionally, risk-hungry investors from across the euro zone may effectively unite to make new issues a feasible

---

* The EU's matching rule for insurance companies, for example, requires foreign currency liabilities to be matched 80 percent by assets in the same currency. Most European pension funds are subject to similar regulations.

F I G U R E 4-3a

Interest rate convergence in Euroland.

Country	1991	1992	1993	1994	1995	1996	1997
Belgium	9.3	8.6	7.2	7.8	7.5	6.5	5.8
Denmark	10.1	10.1	8.8	8.3	8.3	7.2	6.3
Germany	8.6	8.0	6.3	6.7	6.5	5.6	5.1
Spain	12.4	12.2	10.2	9.7	11.0	8.2	5.9
France	9.0	8.6	6.8	7.4	7.5	6.3	5.6
Ireland	9.2	9.1	7.8	8.1	8.3	7.5	6.5
Italy	13.0	13.7	11.3	10.6	11.8	8.9	6.6
Netherlands	8.7	8.1	6.7	7.2	7.2	6.5	5.8
Austria	8.6	8.3	6.6	6.7	7.1	6.3	5.7
Portugal	18.3	15.4	12.5	10.8	10.3	7.3	5.5
Finland	11.7	12.0	8.2	8.4	7.9	6.1	4.9

Source: Eurostat.

financing option. It should come as no surprise that investment banking and consulting firms from around the world are positioning themselves to be a part of this burgeoning market.

Moreover, the Stability & Growth Pact, which limits government budget deficits to 3 percent, ensures that many Euroland governments will be issuing less debt than they have in the past. (Remember, governments need to raise money only when they spend more than they have, that is, when they have a budget deficit.) This in turn may open up the playing field to corporate issuers who previously felt crowded out, because government debt has traditionally accounted for the bulk of Euroland's outstanding debt. Economists and financiers hope that the new trans-European bond market will enable corpora-

FIGURE 4-3b

Interest rate convergence in Euroland. (*Continued*)

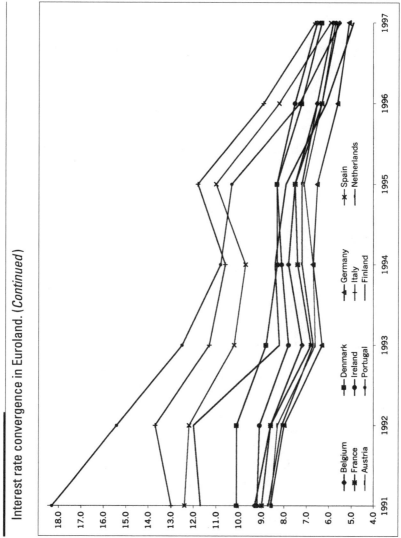

tions, which today rely heavily on bank borrowing, to have access to highly liquid corporate bond markets like those found in the United States. If this occurs, the potential beneficiaries include multinationals around the world.

Of course, none of the euro's effects on bond markets are confined to Europe. Every bond in the world denominated in a national Euroland currency must be paid in euro after 2002. Major international institutions—the World Bank, the European Investment Bank, and International Finance Corporation, for instance—hold about 50 percent of their $311 billion of outstanding debt in European currencies.[48] The conversion of this debt gives the euro roughly the same standing in international debt markets as the U.S. dollar. If the euro continues to attract bond investors from around the world, U.S. issuers may ultimately bear part of the cost through the higher interest rates required to maintain demand for U.S. securities. Even if anything so drastic never occurs, it is clear that the euro revolutionizes the relationship between bond issuers and investors worldwide.

Chapter Summary

- The strength of the euro is determined by a variety of factors. These include (1) the general level of economic and political stability, (2) fiscal stability, (3) the current account balance, (4) inflation and interest rates, and (5) the euro's use as an international reserve currency.

- The euro has already become an important international reserve currency, not least by virtue of the fact that all previous Euroland currencies, regardless of where they are held, converted automatically into euros on January 1, 1999. It is highly unlikely, however, that the euro will pose a serious challenge to the U.S. dollar in the near future.

- The euro's stability is at least as important as its strength. Because the euro transforms Euroland from 11 small, open nations, into one large, closed economy, the ECB is likely to adopt a policy of "benign neglect" toward other currencies like the U.S. dollar. This may ultimately result in volatility similar to that seen in U.S. dollar markets. The first few years of euro trading are likely to be particularly unpredictable, because EMU itself remains shrouded in uncertainty.

- The euro revolutionizes European business markets in many ways. Most important, the new currency (1) reduces financial diversity, (2) conditions pan-European expansion, and (3) promotes market-related policy harmonization. Nonetheless, Euroland remains an extremely heterogeneous place, with 11 distinct governments, legal environments, labor force profiles, and official languages.

- In the short and medium term, the euro does little or nothing to ease Europe's acute unemployment situation, despite a glut of political claims to the contrary. Experts vehemently disagree about the euro's potential long-term impact on unemployment. This controversy underlines one of the euro's greatest ironies: It is totally unclear whether Europe's most sweeping economic policy change in the postwar period will do anything to solve its most acute problem.

- The euro brings important changes to markets around the world. Overnight, the euro has created a whole new set of relationships between European firms and the prices of their goods and services in foreign markets. In the long term, the euro may also (1) increase the cost of U.S. borrowing, (2) become the dominant reserve and transaction currency of countries with close links to the European Union, and (3) enable European firms to use their large internal market as the lever of aggressive foreign expansion.

- The euro is widely expected to promote a general trend of expansion, consolidation, and sophistication that will finally make European stock markets competitive with their American and Japanese counterparts. Moreover, the euro changes the rules of portfolio diversification in European markets and overturns the investment techniques of institutions around the world.

- Overnight, the euro has healed the fractures of Euroland's 11 public debt markets, instantly creating a pool of euro-denominated assets around the globe. Other important changes include (1) the narrowing of interest rate differences and (2) the increased importance of credit and liquidity risk in accounting for these differences. In the long term, the euro lays the foundation for financial innovation and the expansion of corporate debt markets.

C H A P T E R

The Euro's Effects on Firms and Individuals Worldwide

Every public and private institution in the world is well advised to assess its exposure to the European Economic and Monetary Union. Depending on an institution's client base, supplier profile, strategic ambitions, competitive environment, and technological sophistication, the euro presents a range of challenges and opportunities. Indeed, almost no business, from the smallest law firm and investment partnership to the largest multinational, is guaranteed immunity from the euro's effects.

The best way to assess exposure to monetary union is to systematically examine every managerial level of an organization. For those in which European contacts or relationships play even a tangential role, the costs of delay may be very serious:

- Major competitive threats may be ignored.
- Growth opportunities may be squandered.
- Research may become obsolete.
- Legal complications may arise.
- Information systems may malfunction.
- Investment opportunities may be lost.

The purpose of this chapter is to survey the range of opportunities and complications that the euro presents and to provide an overview of the various action items that managers, administrators, investors, researchers, and policymakers need to address. Where the previous chapter discussed business environments, we now turn to industries, firms, and individuals. Complete with a strategic overview and a list of technical complications, this final chapter offers a crash course in the most important firm-level effects of the new trans-European currency.

31. Which industries and firms have the most to gain from the euro?

Years of preparation for the euro have made it abundantly clear that the new currency affects industries unequally. Although the next 10 or 20 years will reveal which global sectors experience the most profound transformations, a few things are already certain.

In general, the euro's biggest winners are those firms or organizations with a high proportion of trade with Euroland countries. This includes businesses from Milan and London to San Francisco and Montreal. Excepting those cases in which the euro is extremely strong or weak compared to one of the preceding national currencies—and has a direct adverse effect on a specific firm's assets, liabilities, or competitive environment—the euro's four core economic benefits are beneficial to firms worldwide (see question 10). Consider the Australian chemical company that prints and sends 11 different versions of its 400-page pricing manual to Europe, manuals that differ only in the currencies stated beside different products. Or the American financial institution that spends tens of millions of dollars managing its European currency hedges. In short, the euro's exchange rate risk, transaction cost, and price transparency–related benefits are a potential boon to any firm that has found itself mired in Europe's pool of national currencies.*

In terms of specific industries, the primary beneficiaries are those directly involved in the euro conversion process. Software firms, electronics manufacturers, printers, graphic designers, and financial advisers, for instance, continue to enjoy a substantial one-time surge in demand, as everything from

---

* Though non-European firms naturally accrue transaction costs on euro conversions, the tremendous size of euro exchange markets ensures low bid-ask spreads on those transactions and thus low costs.

sophisticated security trading models to office supply invoices are adapted to the new currency. As of yet, this trend shows no signs of waning. Indeed, there have been industry reports of serious shortages of software engineers qualified to reprogram precious corporate databases and accounting packages.

Another clear and immediate beneficiary of monetary union is the tourism industry. After January 1, 2002, traveling across Euroland will involve as many trips to *bureaux de change* as a trip from Maine to California. Already, many package tours and price lists have been fully converted into euros, and tourists paying with credit cards may find a single type of foreign currency on their bills. Once euro notes and coins arrive, not only will tourists be spared conversion costs appearing in the form of fees and precious time, they will also benefit from greater price transparency on everything from hotel prices and luxury liner reservations to tour guides and travel books. The hope is that these changes will deliver European tourism to its greatest era. Industry growth predictions mirror this sentiment. Of course, a single currency benefits not only travelers, but also major tour operators worldwide, who have traditionally spent millions of dollars hedging exchange rate exposure on their packages.

Another industry group expected to disproportionately benefit from the euro consists of financial services firms familiar with the opportunities and intricacies of large capital markets. Particularly germane are American and Japanese investment banking and consulting operations, which are in a position to leverage tremendous experience with corporate bonds, asset-backed securities, IPOs, mergers, and acquisitions into the new trans-European financial markets. The natural constraints of 11 smaller national markets have left many European financial institutions at a severe disadvantage in the midst of Euroland's monetary revolution.

32. Which industries and firms are most at risk?

Under the extremely good assumption that the euro proves stable and sustainable, the new currency doesn't produce a lot of surefire losers. Yet a few types of businesses do bear a disproportionate share of the burden.

European firms that need to make significant euro-related transition investments but that don't accrue any of the compensating benefits from international trade, for instance, see little benefit from monetary union. Remember, EMU is a vast project in which organizations are making tremendous up-front investments based on the promise of easier and more efficient international trade and thus greater economic growth. Yet international trade hardly plays a significant role in every European business. Although we live in an era of increasing globalization, never forget that the majority of the world's firms still derive the bulk of their revenue from home markets. With that said, imagine the grocers, bakers, engineers, builders, consultants, and attorneys across Europe who are investing in everything from payroll changes to new cash registers, but who do not benefit from increased international price transparency and reduced exchange rate risk. Even consider the subsidiary of a major multinational with sales and supply operations confined to a single market such as Germany or Finland. The euro's core economic effects appear to offer few significant benefits to such organizations.

The banking sector also bears a disproportionate share of the euro's costs and risks. Though bankers claim that their losses in EMU are outweighed by the euro's long-term benefits, financial institutions are subject to the largest and most immediate business adjustments.

First, as institutions whose primary product is money, banks are particularly affected by euro transition costs. The

European Banking Federation estimates this cost to be about $11 billion a year—roughly 2 percent of the banking sector's total annual operating costs.[49] Second, banks are massively reducing their foreign exchange and hedging operations, because 11 major currencies have instantly become one. While this effect is particularly robust in the European banking sector, it holds for financial institutions worldwide. Third, tighter competition for loans and other financial services is emerging, because a greater variety of banks across Euroland now offer an identical product: euro investment and advising services. Every type of financial product, from Dutch savings accounts to Italian bond underwriting, is thus subject to greater competition.

The natural effect of this is that some banks will become unprofitable, and Euroland is likely to see a substantial medium-term reduction in its enormous number of bank branches. Europe is home to about 10,000 lending institutions, including savings and cooperative banks. After the United States' regulation-driven big bang in the 1970s, its number of lending institutions fell from 15,000 to around 9,000.[50] Judging by the high level of European bank merger activity today, a similar trend is already sweeping Europe.

An excellent way to determine which other sectors are particularly susceptible to the euro's negative effects is to systematically examine specific vulnerabilities to EMU-initiated changes. The industries that are witnessing the most significant and potentially threatening changes are those that (1) need to make large currency management and training investments, (2) are directly involved in currency-related businesses, (3) are vulnerable to cross-border competition, (4) are particularly sensitive to movements in Euroland interest rates, and (5) are directly affected by changes in the size and sophistication of EU capital markets. The consulting firm KPMG, after appraising similar criteria, claims that the insurance, telecommunications, transport, utilities, and pharmaceutical sectors are particularly high-risk areas.[51] Whether these risks are viewed as threats or opportunities, however, can be determined only at the company level.

33. What strategic challenges does the euro present to businesses worldwide?

To many firms, the euro presents an opportunity to reorganize business practices and reorient market strategies. Why? Because the euro permanently changes the basic rules of European business environments and is spurring major competitive moves worldwide. Financial institutions, from the German Bundesbank to America's Chase Manhattan, for instance, have been forced to reorganize international operations out of pure necessity. With the euro's arrival, divisions based on national currencies often become useless. Other firms are seizing the euro less as a defensive maneuver than as a springboard for international expansion.

The euro's strategic impacts are best divided into six general areas: Markets, Competition, Products, Sourcing, Financing, and Organization. Figure 5-1 summarizes the key questions attached to these areas and serves as a checklist for strategic "euro exposure" evaluations.

Markets. Changes in Euroland markets are perhaps the most self-evident. First, trans-European price transparency and a common means of payment make international expansion and distribution easier than ever. Not only have exchange rate risk and currency confusion melted away, but advertising campaigns, catalogs, price lists, packing slips, sales databases, and pricing strategies are much more easily coordinated with a single currency than without one. Second, the euro makes market segmentation considerably more challenging. It is now impossible, for instance, for sales managers to convince clients that published price differences across Euroland borders are due to exchange rate fluctuations and risk. Customers in high-priced market segments may force downward pressure on prices as they actively compare prices abroad.

Competition.   The euro not only makes entry into new European markets more attractive, it also makes existing markets extremely vulnerable. Belgian banks are already raiding customers in northern France with unprecedented vigor.[52] The wonders of electronic commerce and Internet business are encouraging small European exporters to develop aggressive international advertising campaigns. Accordingly, firms judging their own euro exposures are well advised to conduct a similar exercise from the perspective of their competitors.

Products.   The creation of trans-European markets may eventually make large numbers of niche products economically feasible. Restricted domestic demand may not have offered a sufficient customer base to support a particular item or innovation, but the assimilation of all 11 domestic markets under the umbrella of monetary union sheds new light on the cash-flow projections of many closeted business plans. Second, converting prices into euros often results in "unfriendly" euro figures that galvanize product change. A 50-pfennig candy bar, depending on the actual euro exchange rates to be announced on January 1, 1999, may become a 32-euro-cent item. A 99.99-franc office product may convert to 15.67 euros. One possible business response to these ugly conversions, given a retailer's natural aversion to tossing away time-tested "trailing-nine" pricing strategies, is to change the product itself. The candy bar may be made bigger and repriced at 50 euro cents. The office product may be bundled in smaller quantities, or made from cheaper materials, and priced at €14.99.

F I G U R E 5-1

The Euro's Strategic Challenges.

Topic	Sample Questions	Important Considerations
Markets	▪ Is it easier for us to expand into new European markets? ▪ Should we leverage our operations from one Euroland country into others?	▪ Where 11 currencies once existed, there is now one. Euro prices are now quoted from Ireland to Italy.
Competition	▪ Are new competitors, especially those with existing EU operations, likely to enter our markets? ▪ Are our customers now more likely to compare our prices with those of other European competitors? ▪ Do euro exchange rate changes affect our competitors differently than they do us?	▪ Reduced transaction costs and exchange rate risks may spur European expansion. ▪ Competitors may view the euro as a timely opportunity to leverage and expand operations, even if the new currency itself played a subordinate role in the decision.
Products	▪ Do we have to change any characteristics of existing products? ▪ Is there an opportunity to create new products? ▪ How does the euro impact our pricing strategy? ▪ Should euro price changes be used as an opportunity to make non-currency-related price changes?	▪ Financial and information technology (IT) products are particularly susceptible to change. ▪ Price discrimination in different markets may be more difficult to implement. ▪ Direct conversions from national currencies often result in unattractive numbers (9.99 marks may become 4.57 euro).

Sourcing	■ Are multicountry supply chains easier to establish? ■ How has the euro affected the business strategies of our suppliers? ■ Will there be less fluctuation in procurement costs?	■ The euro simplifies competitive price comparisons. ■ The euro reduces some of the complications of importing.
Organization	■ Should we redistribute labor-intensive production to Euroland's low-wage periphery? ■ Should the euro change the organization of our sales force?	■ Organizational divisions along national lines may no longer be logical or efficient.
Financing	■ Does the size of euro lending and equity markets change our financing strategy? ■ Does the euro make it easier for us to offer financing to our customers? ■ How does the euro affect our hedging activities? ■ What level of euro-denominated assets are we willing to expose ourselves to? ■ Are the low euro interest rate levels here to stay?	■ The euro is driving consolidation and expansion in the EU banking sector. ■ European exchange rate risk has an entirely different character than before EMU. ■ Though euro-zone currency movements were correlated before EMU, they are now perfectly correlated, because there is only one currency.

Sourcing.   There is no doubt that the elimination of Euro-land exchange rate fluctuations and currency conversion costs, the emergence of price transparency, and increased competition benefit corporate procurement. Purchasers may be able to put downward pressure on prices in view of newfound import possibilities. Supply tenders may be opened up to foreign bidders for the first time. Supply contracts may no longer need complicated exchange rate clauses. From a strategic perspective, it is the obligation of each business to use the euro as an opportunity to review every single supply arrangement related to a European producer. Even if the euro introduced few new competitors or alternative supply conditions in the short term, the threat of such may still persuade key suppliers to improve the terms of their contracts.

Organization.   Why break up departments along national lines when language-based divisions may function more effectively? A firm's internal organization is affected wherever customer, supplier, or financial relationships partially define departments and hierarchies. Of course, regulatory and cultural environments still differ drastically across Euroland economies. Yet national divisions created because of market segmentation or currency-related issues may already be anachronistic. The euro also increases the feasibility of trans-European production strategies. In the same way that U.S. companies like Ford, Xerox, and IBM manage different elements of research and production across the United States, so European operations are now better able to take advantage of different nations' comparative advantages. It is for precisely this reason that many experts predict that the low-wage economies of Ireland, Italy, Portugal, and Spain will witness unprecedented levels of manufacturing investment over the next decade.

Financing.   Financial consequences break down into two groups. First, the creation of deep trans-European financial markets alters both the range of available financial instruments and the success of individual offerings. Traditional assumptions about the feasibility of corporate bond or public-share issues, for example, may be outdated. Larger Euroland capital markets may simply make some debt and equity instruments less costly than they were before EMU. Second, the euro changes the rules of some corporate treasury activities. Evaluations of any business's ongoing financial strategy, for instance, needs to consider (1) the elimination of some hedging activities, (2) the arrival of a new currency risk profile (with euro-related risk supplanting distinct national currency risks), and (3) opportunities to manage cash more efficiently.

34. What technical challenges does the euro present to businesses worldwide?

Although strategic aspects of Economic and Monetary Union certainly have the most lasting impacts, the euro's technical complications should not be taken lightly. Because the euro potentially affects every operational layer of a business, managers are advised to begin the internal review process immediately.

The best way to approach a "euro exposure" review is to literally list every operational element of an organization and to ask whether the arrival of a new currency affects each item. Start from the top, identifying areas in sales, billing, production, shipping, inventory, purchasing, administration, communications, information systems, research, and human resources. Then proceed downward through the organization until every piece of hardware and software in the business that is related to European operations, from accounting packages to postage machines, has been inspected for euro compatibility. Though some technical complications (e.g., those concerning cash registers and postage machines) are relevant only to firms with physical operations in Euroland, many others (e.g., product pricing) affect businesses worldwide. It is crucial to allot sufficient time for internal review as well as for follow-up testing and training.

Figure 5-2 serves as a checklist for the technical review process. Though it covers diverse subjects, two general questions emerge: (1) Can systems technically process euro-denominated transactions? (2) Does the euro offer opportunities to improve operations? It is worth elaborating a few features in each of these areas.

Processing euro transactions.   Even businesses that do nothing but import into or export out of Euroland—or that accept payment in one of the region's 11 national currencies—may need to ensure that price lists, packing slips, invoices, receipts, software, operating systems, web sites, bank accounts, accounting packages, and sales or purchasing reports are equipped to handle euros. Invoices may cost thousands of dollars to redesign and print. Price lists worldwide will soon become obsolete. Some Internet ads will soon show their obsolescence by referring to incorrect currencies. Software challenges, though often supported by professional software designers, should not be discounted. Microsoft Corporation's official procedure for installing the euro currency symbol, €, in its popular office productivity programs (including Word and Excel) is four pages long and anything but straightforward. Similarly, few computer keyboards currently have the € symbol installed as a typeable character.

For firms with physical operations in Euroland, such problems can be particularly acute. Cash registers need to handle multiple currencies during the Phase C transition period. Postage machines need to print euro values, and vending machines of all kinds need to be reengineered. In such cases, individual product suppliers should be contacted immediately.

Efficiency gains.   Any internal business review must also examine opportunities to increase efficiency. Because the euro completely replaces 11 currencies, it may streamline electronic data processing (EDP) and cash management logistics. Depending on the organization, the euro may encourage account consolidation, reports, synchronization, sales centralization, and document streamlining. Of course, large multinationals may still be plagued by as many as 15 different European currencies, from the euro and pound to the zloty and krona. Nonetheless, any organization accepting the euro's costs without evaluating its potential benefits unnecessarily condemns itself to an unsuccessful experience with monetary union.

35. What accounting challenges does the euro present to businesses worldwide?

The euro's impact on the accounting profession can be divided into three central areas: accounting systems, adoption costs, and financial reporting. Euro-initiated changes to *accounting systems* are the most direct and immediate. Specifically, accounting departments need to analyze which accounts are likely to be affected by euro values and then prepare them to handle ongoing transactions in the new currency. Problems may arise where (1) historical values need to be restated in euros, (2) a single account needs to handle euros and national currencies simultaneously, or (3) accounts need to be permanently redenominated in euros. For a large international organization, all three of these problems are likely to arise.

For firms with only incidental euro transactions, a straightforward if cumbersome approach is to simply continue operating with national currency denominations and then to convert final balances to euros using the permanent, fixed exchange rates to be published on January 1, 1999. Firms with extensive

F I G U R E 5-2

The Euro's technical challenges.

Topic	Sample Questions	Important Considerations
Advertising	▪ How far ahead of time do we need to notify our catalog printers or advertisers of a new pricing regime?	▪ Though language differences still splinter pan-European campaigns, the euro may present opportunities for advertising consolidation.
Information processing	▪ Do all necessary software programs, from statistical macros to word processors, support the euro? ▪ Is there a clearly defined section of the intranet devoted to euro policies?	▪ Few keyboards and software programs are euro-compatible. ▪ Vendors should be contacted early in the event that code needs to be revised.
Inventory	▪ Are we prepared to physically reprice old inventory after Phase B? ▪ How and when will we reprice our existing inventory data records?	▪ Without a clear transition strategy, identical items may accidentally be listed in multiple currencies.
Labeling and packaging	▪ Are we prepared to produce price lists, labels, and packing slips in multiple currencies during Phase B?	▪ Phase B of EMU is characterized by a dual-pricing period of up to three years.

Machines and devices	■ Are all relevant devices in Euroland, from postage meters to cash counters, equipped to handle the euro?	■ Few existing machines are euro-compatible.
Payroll	■ Is the salary or pension component of any employee's compensation currently paid in Euroland currencies?	■ Salaries must be fully converted by the end of Phase B.
Training	■ Are our employees aware of the euro and its consequences? ■ Are our employees capable of processing multiple currencies during Phase C?	■ The euro potentially affects operations at all levels, from data entry to inventory management.
Transactions	■ Will any of our suppliers invoice in euros? If so, when will they start? ■ Should we start invoicing in euros?	■ No one can be forced to pay in euros before the end of Phase B. The sooner mutual agreements are established, however, the easier the transition process.

Euroland business may need to invest in a multicurrency accounting system capable of expressing any given value in any account in either of several equivalent denominations at any given time. This is no small task and is particularly important for firms accepting payment in national currencies and euros simultaneously. Imagine a firm that invoices in euro but is paid in francs—a perfectly legal transaction during Phase B. In the absence of preprogrammed euro-tolerance levels, small rounding differences in booking the two sides of this transaction may raise error signals. In some cases, customized multicurrency accounting software may need to be installed.

The second major euro-related accounting question regards *transition costs*. Are such costs incurred in a single year, or are they to be depreciated? In the EU, treatment defaults to the individual regulations of member countries, and businesses reporting there should contact their accounting authorities immediately. In the United States, the Federal Accounting Standards Bureau (FASB) issued a clear opinion on May 21, 1998, that states, "The staff believes that not all costs associated with upgrading or replacing computer software and costs to make physical modifications to fixed assets to accommodate the introduction of the Euro necessarily should be expenses as incurred. The staff believes that those costs should be accounted for in accordance with the entity's existing accounting policies for similar costs." In other words, euro-adoption expenses cannot necessarily be expensed in one year and need to follow currently employed procedures. The FASB expects to issue more euro-related opinions in the near future.

Finally, *financial reporting* worldwide needs to reflect the introduction of a trans-European unit of account. First, by the end of Phase B, any and all financial statements (including statement footnotes) featuring Euroland currency denominations need to be stated in euros. This act alone affects prospec-

tuses, business plans, federal and state security filings, tax forms, shareholder letters, annual reports, and press releases throughout a business. It is advisable to convert all financial reports simultaneously, as conflicting figures in different publications only confuse audiences. Second, for firms filing their statements in euros, historical recasting needs to follow specific guidelines. In the United States, for instance, the SEC issued a July 23, 1998, opinion (Topic No. D-71) for firms changing their reporting currency to the euro that lists the specific requirements of euro-related financial statement recasting. The report's fundamental conclusion is that "the staff will not object if a registrant presents comparative financial statements for periods prior to January 1, 1999, by recasting previously reported financial statements into Euros using the exchange rate between the Euro and the prior reporting currency as of January 1, 1999." Some very specific requirements apply to this process, and accountants are urged to order the short SEC report as soon as possible.

36. How should managers handle the euro's arrival?

Adapting a business to the euro can be a daunting task. Though the average business is spared the need for euro task forces and executive committees, a few easy guidelines can streamline the "euro exposure" evaluation process in organizations of all sizes.

First, it is advisable to appoint a euro project leader, even if currency-related issues play only a small role in the organization. Ideally, this person is in a relatively high executive position and has access to and knowledge of a range of divisions or departments. Though the euro project leader needn't conduct individual departmental analyses, he or she should serve as a focal point for the full range of case studies, statistics, and

internal evaluations that ultimately become part of a company's final euro report.

The second step involves the formulation of project teams split along business divisions or subject lines. These "teams" may consist of a single person, responsible for a specific area such as software, cash management, or advertising, but it is crucial that the project leader not create a euro evaluation in a vacuum. The input of managers and administrators throughout an organization is absolutely essential. Outside consultants, of course, may also play an important role. Expert-level advice from marketing professionals, traders, IT managers, and attorneys may very well be necessary if euro-related problems are expected to reach an unmanageable scale.

Finally, effective managers remember from the very beginning that euro adoption procedures may require considerable time and training to implement and test. Price changes, product designs, advertising campaigns, or software upgrades, for example, are often best taken care of in the natural replacement cycles in these areas. Why force a business into expensive last-minute software upgrades in 2001 when the problem could have been uneventfully solved years earlier? It is also worth pointing out that the distribution of the results and recommendations of an internal euro review are useful only if they are widely distributed. It is precisely for this reason that euro-savvy companies, including Nokia, Siemens, and BMW, devote sizable portions of their intranets to the euro and its organizational challenges.

37. What legal problems does the euro present to businesses worldwide?

Over the next several years, anyone on the losing end of a business agreement may well be tempted to claim that the intro-

duction of a new currency frees them from their financial commitments. Prospectuses, business plans, derivatives, loans, leases, and project financings, to name only a few types of agreements, commonly make direct references to payment in specific national currencies. But if a contractually specified currency like the mark or lira *no longer exists,* doesn't that automatically frustrate thousands of such business agreements worldwide?

The European Union has passed two crucial regulations to deal with legal questions of this nature. The first, "Council Regulation on Some Provisions Relating to the Introduction of the Euro," based on Article 235 of the Treaty on European Union, became law on June 20, 1997. It clearly states that the euro "shall not have the effect of altering any term of a legal instrument or of discharging or excusing performance under any legal instrument, nor give a party the right unilaterally to alter or terminate such an instrument." The second, "Council Regulation on the Introduction of the Euro," based on Article 1091(4) of the Treaty on European Union, addresses the interchangeability of national currencies and the euro. It says that any references to marks or lira, for example, may simply be interpreted as euros instead. The main point of these regulations is to ensure the *continuity of contracts* under EMU. These two regulations state that any contract or agreement that mentions one of Euroland's national currencies, provided it was written under the law of a Euroland country, still holds in full.

These and other regulations contain scores of related clauses and stipulations, but businesses can use five guiding principles to begin their assessments.

- As of January 1, 1999, contractual references to a national Euroland currency legally refer to an equivalent number of euros, as determined by the official and permanent euro exchange rates announced shortly before that date. National currencies are therefore mere "expressions" of the euro.

- Agreements that cite a specific payment currency continue to be fulfilled in that currency until the end of Phase B, unless the parties agree otherwise. A business cannot, for instance, fulfill a franc contract by making euro payments until the end of Phase B, unless the parties have explicitly agreed that payments may be made in euros. Phase B is currently set to end on January 1, 2002.

- After 2002, parties are required to settle contracts or agreements exclusively in euros. Hence, a contract written on March 15, 1998, calling for payment in francs should be settled in francs until the end of Phase B but must be settled in euros thereafter.

- Any costs of adapting transactions to the euro are to be handled by the holders of the relevant accounts. Hence, a business would be responsible for changing its price lists, invoices, and receipts to euros, but its customers would be responsible for ensuring that their banks are capable of converting and transferring money in euros.

- EU regulations on euro convertibility are subject to anything to which parties agree. Two businesses may mutually agree in writing, for instance, that the arrival of the euro terminates a contract.

There are two complications that these principles do not address. The first concerns references to the European Currency Unit (Ecu). The Ecu is a composite currency based on a fixed basket of 12 national EU currencies, but which does not exist in note and coin form itself. Created by the European

Monetary System in the late 1970s, it is primarily used as a unit of account for the implementation of economic and monetary policy in Europe. It also appears in many contracts.

EU regulations have purposefully been designed to ensure that the Ecu converts into the euro on a one-to-one basis. That is, any contract calling for payment of one Ecu now calls for the payment of one euro. Generally speaking, only when an agreement explicitly defines the term Ecu as meaning something other than defined by the European Union do exceptions apply.

The second possible contractual complication of the euro concerns floating interest rates. Though EU regulations clearly state that nominal fixed interest rates (e.g., an 8 percent bond coupon payment) are totally unaffected by the introduction of a new currency, floating-rate references are not as clear cut. Floating-rate references, like the London Interbank Offered Rate (Libor), permeate financial contracts and are generally based on the interest rates banks charge each other in the money markets. So what happens to references to mark Libor or escudo Libor? What will happen to the popularly quoted sterling Libor if England joins the single-currency area in 2002?

Unfortunately, the answers to these questions are likely to be determined by mutual agreements and in courtrooms, because EU regulations do not, as of yet, cite a specific set of replacement reference rates. It is important to know, however, that many Euroland floating-rate references have been replaced by newly created equivalents. Though free markets and courtroom decisions will ultimately decide which rate becomes the "new Libor," two contenders have already emerged. The first, known as Euro Libor, is published by the British Bankers Association and is based on the average lending rates of 16 highly creditworthy banks. It is perfectly analogous to previous Libors based on national currencies and is calculated and published by the same organization. The second major euro-based floating–interest rate benchmark is known as the European-Inter-Bank Offer Rate (Euribor), published by the Banking Federation and Association Cambiste Internationale. *Euribor is not the same as Euro Libor.* It is based on the lending rates of 57 European banks. Because it involves a larger number of banks, which are not all as credit-worthy as the 16 banks of its counterpart, it is generally higher than Euro Libor. Businesses need to decide for themselves which of these (or other) variable rates offers the best substitute for those contracts that mention national Euroland currencies.

Countries generally recognize the currency laws of their trading partners, but it should be pointed out that EU law cannot be invoked in courts unless contracts have been explicitly negotiated under its auspices. For this reason, some U.S. states have already passed their own legislation concerning the introduction of the euro.

New York has passed an amendment to Article 5 of its "General Obligations Law." Illinois instituted a "Euro Conversion Act." And California passed Assembly Bill 185 regarding "Interpretation of Contracts: European Currency." The laws of these three states are said to cover the majority of U.S. financial contracts with references to European currencies, and they generally mirror EU regulations guaranteeing the full continuity of contracts after the euro's arrival, though firms should request these documents immediately for clarification. In fact, all of the euro-related laws mentioned in this section warrant professional counsel and specific legal advice.

38. How do euro conversions work?

In May of 1998, a high-level EU committee announced the permanent bilateral exchange rates of EMU's 11 participating nations. They are shown in Figure 5-3. Though the listed Euro-land exchange rates fluctuated significantly in the past, one German mark is now forever worth 102.505 escudos, and 1000 Italian lira are permanently valued at 7.10657 shillings.

Unfortunately, euro conversion rates are not available for the current edition of this book, because they can be determined only by using external trading values of the euro on the last trading day of 1998. As a result, the best way to perform currency conversions between national currencies and the euro on or after January 1, 1999, is to look up the euro values in a major financial newspaper (e.g., the *Wall Street Journal* or the *Financial Times*). Once exchange rates between national currencies and the euro are published, they are locked into place indefinitely.

It is important to point out several particularities of euro currency conversions that must be observed after these official rates are published. First, all conversion rates, including those in Figure 5-3, are stated to six significant figures.* This is not accidental. EU regulations require that all currency conversions be calculated with numbers of exactly this accuracy. It is forbidden to round conversion rates, so it is advisable to ensure that they are programmed into relevant software packages with their full accuracy.

Second, EU regulations technically require that all conversions between one national currency and another be performed using the euro exchange rates as intermediaries. It is forbidden, for instance, to translate directly from German marks to Italian lira using the "990.002" shown in Figure 5-3,

---

* Note that "six significant figures" does not necessarily mean six figures behind the decimal. According to Merriam-Webster, a significant figure is "one of the digits of a number beginning with the digit farthest to the left that is not zero and ending with the last digit farthest to the right that is not zero or is a zero considered to be exact." Hence 0.000001 has only one significant figure, while 20.6255 has six.

FIGURE 5-3

The bilateral exchange rates of EMU.

	German mark	Belgian franc	Spanish paseta	French franc	Irish punt	Italian lira (1000)	Dutch guilder	Austrian schilling	Portuguese escudo
Belgian franc	20.6255								
Spanish paseta	85.0722	4.12462							
French franc	3.35386	.166080	.0394237						
Irish punt	.402676	.0195232	.00473335	.120063					
Italian lira	990.002	47.9990	11.6372	295.163	2458.56				
Dutch guilder	1.12674	.0546285	.0132445	.335953	2.79812	1.13812			
Austrian schilling	7.03552	.341108	.0827006	2.09774	17.4719	7.10657	6.24415		
Portuguese escudo	102.505	4.96984	1.20492	30.5634	254.560	103.541	90.9753	14.5697	
Finnish markka	3.04001	.147391	.0357345	.906420	7.54951	3.07071	2.69806	.432094	.0296571

Source: ECOFIN.

Note: Do not use these bilateral exchange rates to convert directly between two national currencies (e.g., between marks and lira). For the precise and legally sanctioned conversion method, see discussion in question 38.

because using the bilateral rates alone may result in rounding errors. The legally sanctioned method of performing a mark-lira conversion is to (1) convert the marks into euro, rounding this result to no fewer than three decimal places, and then (2) convert this euro figure into lira. The same goes for conversions between any of the two currencies listed in Figure 5-3. This process is known as *triangulation* because it involves three currencies: the starting currency, the euro, and the destination currency.

Rounding rules also follow strict guidelines. First, as mentioned, the intermediate euro conversion step in all "national currency to national currency" conversions must be accurate to at least three decimal places. Second, any final conversion result must be rounded to the nearest subunit of a currency. German marks, for instance, round to the nearest pfennig, francs to the nearest cent. But lira simply round to the nearest lira, because the Italian currency has no subunits. Also, as is typical in financial practice, numbers ending in 5 or above round up, so that 0.005 rounds to 0.01.

39. How should investors approach the new currency?

First and foremost, investors should never underestimate the incredible and persistent diversity of European markets and economies, even with the advent of Economic and Monetary Union. The primary industries, import and export ratios, savings rates, growth rates, regulatory environments, supply and demand profiles, and democratic styles of the 11 current EMU participants vary dramatically. Figure 5-4 shows (in both table and graph form) Euroland stock market performances since 1990. Note that firms in Finland's timber- and telecommunications-dependent economy are subject to a significantly different set of opportunities and risks than those in

Austria. Despite a common currency, investors will always be able to achieve superior returns by correctly pinpointing those individual Euroland economies that are poised to outstrip their counterparts.

Second, investors need to be aware that Euroland capital markets are undergoing greater change than at any other time in the past century (see questions 29 and 30). Most important, the size and sophistication of stock, bond, and derivatives markets across the continent are expected to increase dramatically over the next decade as (1) a common currency eliminates much of the risk and uncertainty of cross-border investments; (2) government bond markets shrink due to Stability Pact borrowing restrictions, opening up the field for new types of investments and higher personal savings; and (3) young European investors eschew Europe's traditionally risk-averse nature and embrace high-return securities. Accordingly, expect big growth in European private equity opportunities, small-cap IPOs, high-grade corporate bonds, junk bonds, and asset-backed securities.

This brings us to an important related point: Euro-initiated investing benefits are not confined to European investors. International investors worldwide now find that they bear a single type of currency risk in Euroland: euro risk against their home currencies. American investors, for example, find that their existing investments in European mutual funds vary with exchange rate fluctuations in a different manner than previously. After all, the value of one share of Fiat no longer hinges on the lira's value against the U.S. dollar. Only the dollar-euro exchange rate matters. In this way, foreign investors are finding themselves more inclined to invest in Euroland countries with traditionally volatile currencies because the euro promises a more stable future for many of these nations. The euro itself offers a totally new, broad-based currency investment opportunity. Indeed, portfolio managers from Beijing to London have already revealed plans to diversify enormous portions of their foreign currency portfolios into euros. Individual investors are expected to follow.

The third major euro-initiated change in investment communities concerns investment professionals themselves. Because the euro imposes a common type of exchange rate risk in Euroland, security analysts, brokers, and fund managers are expected to institute a bottom-up approach to regional investing (see question 29). If the entire Euroland region now shares a common exchange rate risk, why invest by selecting countries first and particular investments second, as funds have often done in the past? Indeed, a Merrill Lynch survey finds that 71 percent of fund managers think that EMU will make them rely more on "sector plays" than on country-based approaches.[53]

Regardless of which industrial sectors suit an investor's interests, investors need to devote serious thought to the euro's long-term success. Put simply, more-liquid markets, new financial instruments, and the elimination of currency confusion are all negligible gains if long-term investors do not believe that monetary union will survive the next major economic shock and recession (see question 15). If the euro does bring the incredible long-term-growth benefits promised by its proponents, then there is no better time than now to invest in pan-European blue-chip companies. These firms not only benefit enormously from a higher European growth trajectory, but also, as major exporters, benefit disproportionately from the euro's core economic effects. New indices have been designed to capture the returns of Euroland's blue-chip giants. The Euro Stoxx 50, for example, is now the "Dow Jones" of the EU and is in fact published by that company. Dow Jones also offers the more general Euro Stoxx index, which includes hundreds of firms rather than

FIGURE 5-4a

Euroland share price performances.

Country	1990	1991	1992	1993	1994	1995	1996	1997
Belgium	100	92.6	91.1	100.6	112.2	109.8	132.3	176.8
Denmark	100	108.1	99.0	101.1	120.6	120.5	147.7	194.5
Germany	100	91.5	87.1	93.2	106.2	103.6	118.2	162.0
Spain	100	102.7	89.0	104.8	121.5	114.5	142.0	215.0
France	100	113.1	116.9	130.1	137.8	120.0	136.3	182.1
Ireland	100	89.7	83.2	104.5	118.4	129.8	162.0	221.0
Italy	100	85.5	69.9	83.5	104.1	95.4	96.0	131.5
Netherlands	100	103.7	108.5	128.0	149.1	157.1	205.0	305.8
Austria	100	84.9	67.5	67.4	75.5	65.6	69.7	79.0
Portugal	100	85.6	75.1	88.6	116.2	111.6	130.9	202.7
Finland	100	72.4	58.4	93.2	139.0	144.0	153.5	241.0

Source: Eurostat.
Note: Figures are based on annual share price index averages, except those for Germany, Ireland, and Austria, which are based on end-of-year data.

F I G U R E 5-4b

Euroland share price performances. (*Continued*)

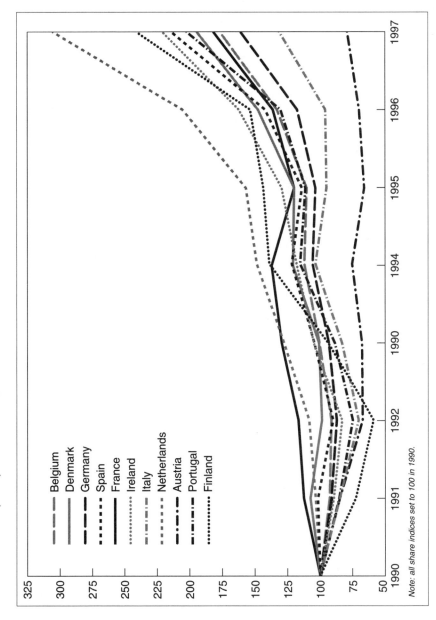

Note: all share indices set to 100 in 1990.

155

just fifty. The *Financial Times* also issues its popular FTSE Euratop 300 index, and Morgan Stanley publishes its MCSI indices. These trans-European indices include Euroland giants such as Societé Générale, Siemens, ING, Philips, Telecom Italia, and Bayer.

Chapter Summary

- All industries and firms do not share the same exposure to EMU. In the short term, those firms best poised to take full advantage of the euro are (1) businesses with a high proportion of trade with Euroland countries, (2) those directly involved in the transition process, (3) those in the tourism industry, and (4) finance companies with expertise in large and enormously liquid markets.

- A few industries carry a disproportionate share of EMU's risks. Particularly at risk are European firms that need to make substantial euro-related investments but that conduct little international trade. Other at-risk industries include the banking, insurance, telecommunications, transport, utilities, and pharmaceutical sectors.

- The euro permanently changes the basic rules of European business environments and is spurring competitive repositioning worldwide. The new currency's strategic impacts can be divided into six general areas: Markets, Competition, Products, Sourcing, Financing, and Organization.

- The euro potentially affects every operational layer of a business, from software upgrades and keyboard replacement to inventory management and control.

Businesses are advised to begin the internal review process immediately. The technical evaluation process needs to acknowledge (1) complications in processing euro transactions, (2) new challenges unrelated to individual transactions, and (3) opportunities to enhance efficiency.

- The euro's effects on the accounting profession can be broken into three central areas: those on (1) accounting systems, (2) adoption costs, and (3) financial reporting.

- Though many businesses are spared the need for euro task forces and executive committees, a few easy guidelines can streamline the "euro exposure" evaluation process in organizations of all sizes. Most important, businesses should (1) appoint a euro project manager, (2) draw on the expertise and experiences of employees at all levels, and (3) allot sufficient time for testing and training periods needed to institute euro-initiated changes.

- The European Union has passed two crucial regulations to address legal questions that the euro presents. Though the transition period poses a unique set of challenges, every effort has been made to ensure the continuity of contracts and agreements, despite the complete disappearance of currencies upon which they may be based.

- The best way to perform currency conversions between national currencies and the euro on or after January 1, 1999, is to look up the permanent euro exchange values that will appear in major financial newspapers such as the *Wall Street Journal* or the *Financial Times.* It is important to note that the EU has issued a specific set of conversion and rounding

rules that define the legal method of currency
conversion.

- The euro overturns many traditional assumptions about
  European investing. Most important, investors should
  (1) expect big growth in European private equity
  opportunities, small-cap IPOs, high-grade corporate
  bonds, junk bonds, and asset-backed securities, (2)
  recognize that the relationship between currency
  movements and investment returns in Euroland has
  permanently changed, (3) acknowledge the existence
  of a new investment currency, and (4) prepare for a
  reorientation in fund managers' approaches to
  European investments.

APPENDIX

For those readers interested in more in-depth information on the changeover to the euro and the effects on the worldwide economic community, a plethora of material is available from European central banks, as well as on the World Wide Web. Most of the following sites have information in English. Here is just a sampling of where to look.

CENTRAL BANKS

Banco de España
> http://www.bde.es/ume/ume.htm
>> An English version of this page is provided at the Internet address http://www.bde.es/ume/umee.htm.

Banco de Portugal
> http://www.bportugal.pt/document/frdocument_p.htm
>> This is the euro web page of the Banco de Portugal, the Portuguese central bank.

Bank of England
> http://www.bankofengland.co.uk/publica.htm#europe
>> The web site containing a series of reports entitled "Practical issues arising from the introduction of the euro" published by the Bank of England.

Banque de France
> http://www.banque-france.fr/actu/europe/eurindex.htm
>> This is the euro web page of the Banque de France, the French central bank. You'll find an English version of the web site at http://www.banque-france.fr/us/home.htm.

Danmarks Nationalbank
> http://www.nationalbanken.dk
>> The web site of Danmarks Nationalbank, the Danish central bank.

De Nederlandsche Bank
> http://www.dnb.nl/emufrmset.htm
>> The euro Web page of De Nederlandsche Bank offers information in Dutch about EMU, the ECB, and the euro.

Deutsche Bundesbank
> http://www.bundesbank.de/de/presse/wwu/eurokommt.htm

This is the euro web page of the Deutsche Bundesbank, the German central bank (in German). You'll find the English version at the Internet address http://www.bundesbank.de/en/presse/wwu/eurokommt.htm.

Oesterreichische Nationalbank
    http://www.Austria.EU.net/oenb/uww01.htm
    The euro web page of the Oesterreichische Nationalbank, the Austrian national bank, is intended to support the euro information campaign for the general public. It contains a brochure for the general public entitled "So wird der Schilling zu Euro."

Suomen Pankki
    http://www.bof.fi/env/eng/kasi/lista.stm
    This is the euro web page of Suomen Pankki, the Finnish central bank.

Sveriges Riksbank
    http://www.riksbank.se/eng/
    The web page, in English, of Sveriges Riksbank, the Swedish central bank, is available at http://www.riksbank.se/textmaterial/pressmed.eng/nya/nro5.doc II.

EU INSTITUTIONS

Esprit Programme
    http://www.ispo.cec.be/y2keuro/scr/y2kbody.htm
    This is the web site of the European Commission (as part of the Esprit project) on "Year 2000 and the euro: IT challenges of the century."

European Commission
    http://europa.eu.int/euro
    This is the euro web site of the European Commission (in all official languages).

European Parliament
    http://www.europarl.eu.int/euro/en/2_pe/default_.htm
    The euro web page of the European Parliament, this site contains information in all the official languages of the EU about the role of the European Parliament in the EMU process and about the Parliament's view of EMU.

NATIONAL GOVERNMENTS

Austrian Federal Ministry of Finance
    http://www.bmwa.gv.at/bmwa/aktuell/top.htm
    This is the euro web page of the Austrian Federal Ministry of Finance.

Euro-Initiative of the Austrian Ministry of Finance
    http://www.euro.gv.at
    This is the web site of the "Euro-Initiative" of the Austrian Ministry of Finance.

Belgian Federal Government
  http://euro.fgov.be/
    This euro web page of the Belgian government explains the changeover to the
    euro (in French, Dutch, English, and German).

Belgian Ministry of Finance
  http://minfin.fgov.be
    This is the euro web site of the Belgian Ministry of Finance in Dutch and
    French.

Dutch Ministry of Finance
  http://www.minfin.nl/europa/europa.htm
    This is the euro web site of the Dutch Ministry of Finance.

Dutch National Forum
  http://www.euro.nl/HOMEFR.htm
    This is the web site of the Dutch National Forum for the introduction of the
    euro.

Finnish Ministry of Finance
  http://www.vn.fi/vm/english/mof.htm
    This is the euro web page in English of the Finnish Ministry of Finance
    (equivalent pages are available in Finnish and Swedish).

Finnish Council of State
  http://www.vn.fi/english/vn7e.htm
    This is the EU site of the Finnish Council of State (in English).

French Ministry of Economic Affairs, Finance, and Industry
  http://www.finances.gouv.fr/euro/index-d.htm
    France—Ministère des Finances et de l'Economie. Euro: le passage à
    monnaie unique (Menu). This is the euro web site of the French
    Government

French Minting Authority
  http://www.monnaiedeparis.fr/francais/info/euro.html
    This is the euro web page of the "Monnaie de Paris," the minting authority of
    France. It includes information on euro coins.

French National Assembly
  http://www.assemblee-nat.fr/
    This is the web site of the French Assemblée Nationale, on which the minutes
    of debates related to the changeover to the euro are available.

German Federal Ministry of Finance
  http://www.bundesfinanzministerium.de/broschueren__online/euro/euro_inhalt
  .htm
    This is the web site of the German Federal Ministry of Finance.

German Federal Ministry of Justice
  http://www.bundesregierung.de/inland/ministerien/bmj_rahmen.html

This page contains the draft legislation for the introduction of the single currency in the German legal system, which has been approved by the German government and is currently being examined by the German Parliament.

Irish Ministry of Finance
http://www.irlgov.ie/finance/225e38a.htm
This is the euro web page of the Irish government (Department of Finance—Ann Roinn Airgeadais), where the Irish National Changeover Plan is published.

Irish Parliament
http://www.irlgov.ie
The Irish Parliament's web site contains the minutes of debates, available under the section entitled "debates."

Irish Revenue Commissioners
http://www.revenue.ie/euro/docstart.htm
This is the euro web page of the tax administration of Ireland (the Revenue Commissioners), from which it is possible to download a business guide on the taxation and customs aspects of the changeover to the euro, entitled "Preparing for the euro" (as a PDF or as a Word file).

Italian Ministry of Treasury, Budget, and Planning
http://www.tesoro.it/euro-sm.htm
This is the euro web site of the Italian Ministry of Treasury, Budget, and Planning.

Italian Ministry of Education
http://eurolandia.tin.it/euro/

Luxembourg Ministry of Finance
http://www.etat.lu/FI/

Portuguese Ministry of Finance's Comissão Euro
http://www.min-financas.pt/Euro/index.html

Spanish Ministry of Economic Affairs and Finance
http://www.euro-mech.org

Swedish Ministry of Finance
http://www.sb.gov/info_rosenbad/department/finans/ds9

UK Treasury
http://www.hm-treasury.gov.uk/pub/html/docs/emu/main.html
This is the EMU practical information page of the UK Treasury.

ASSOCIATIONS OF THE BANKING AND FINANCIAL INDUSTRY

Association Cambiste Internationale
http://www.fxweek.com/aci/eurostat.htm

This is the euro web page of the Association Cambiste Internationale, which contains the joint statement on market conventions for the euro, approved by a number of financial market associations across the EU in July 1997.

Belgian Bankers' Association
http://www.abb-bvb.be/euro/
This is the Belgian Bankers' Association's euro web page (in Flemish and French). It contains a large number of surveys in French and Flemish, including the reports of national-level working groups and the Belgian changeover plan.

European Mortgage Federation
http://www.eu-mortgage-fed.be/Eurouk.html
This is the euro web page of the European Mortgage Federation. It offers expert group reports, euro-related information in connection with mortgages, and information on euro-related conferences.

European Savings Banks Group
http://www.savings-banks.com/esdghome
This is the web site of the European Savings Banks Group, part of which is dedicated to the euro.

French Banking Association
http://www.afb.fr/broceuro.htm
This is the euro web page of the Association Française des Banques, or French Banking Association.

German Association of Co-operative Banks
http://www.vrnet.de/cgi-bin/softweb/EuroKonkret.html

German Banking Association
http://www.bankenverband.de/Presse/EuroFK/Index.htm

International Swaps and Derivatives Association
http://www.isda.org/f1emu.html

Italian Association of Co-operative Banks
http://www.bcc.it/euro/index.html

Italian Association of Private Banks
http://www.assbank.it/_private/_aggiornamenti/txtnovco.htm#ind6

Spanish Banking Community
http:www.geocities.com/WallStreet/8999/cheques.html

CREDIT INSTITUTIONS

ABN Amro Bank
http://www.abnamro.nl/euro/

Allied Irish Banks
http://www.iol.ie/~aibtreas/monthly.htm

Anhyp Banque
http://www.anhyp.be/documentatie/html/euro_fr.html
This is the euro web page of Anhyp Banque of Belgium.

Bacob Banque
http://bacob.webware.be/bacob/fr/euro.html
This is the euro web page of Bacob Banque of Belgium. It consists of 50 questions and answers on the euro for the general public.

Baden-Württembergische Bank
http://www.bw-bank.de/
This is the euro web page of the Baden-Württembergische Bank AG of Germany. It contains information on the euro for retail customers and corporations, including some strategies for investment.

Banca Commerciale Italiana
http://bci.it/ufficio_studi/euro/index.html

Banca di Roma
http://www.bancaroma.it:9090/

Banca Popolare FriulAdria
http://www.friuladria.it/euro/

Banco Ambrosiano
http://www.ambro.it/

Banco Bilbao Vizcaya
http://www.bbv.es/BBV/producto/europyme/noticias.htm

Banco Central Hispano
http://www.bch.es/es/products/euro.html
This is the euro web site of Banco Central Hispano of Spain.

Banco Comercial Português
http://194.79.83.35/euro/bcp.body.html
This is the euro web page of the Portuguese bank Banco Comercial Português. It contains, among other things, a "questions and answers" section, and information on euro banknotes and coins.

Banco Espirito Santo
http://www.bes.pt/euro/euro_intro_toc.html

Banco Português do Atlântico
http://194.79.83.35/euro/atlantico/body.html

Banesto
http://www.banesto.es/empresas/castella/indeurov.htm

Bank Austria
http://www.bankaustria.com/t-cgi-bin/navigator.pl?Navigator=%2Ft-infotainment%2Feu%2Feu5.htm

Bank Nederlandse Gemeenten
http://www.bng.nl/bng/euro/

Bank of Ireland
   http://www.treasury.boi.ie/
      This is the Bank of Ireland's home page (not to be confused with the Central
      Bank of Ireland).

Bankgesellschaft Berlin
   http://www.bankgesellschaft.de/wirtschaftsnews/index.html

Bankinter
   http://www.bankinter.es/particul/euro/indice.htm

Banque et Caisse d'Epargne de l'Etat de Luxembourg
   http://www.bcee.lu/bcee/french/chap0800.htm

Banque Financière Groupama
   http://www.bfg.fr/

Banque Internationale à Luxembourg
   http://www.bil.lu/Euro_fr/default.htm

Banque Nationale de Paris
   http://www.bnp.fr/htm/iguide1.htm

Banque Populaire de Lorraine
   http:www.bplorraine.fr/htm/unique.htm

Barclays Bank
   http://www.barclays.pt/07/07intro.html

Bayerische Hypobank
   http://www.hypo.de/news/euro/index.html

Bilbao Bizkaia Kutxa
   http://www.bbk.es/esp/euro/index.html
      This is the euro web site of Bilbao Bizkaia Kutxa, the Spanish savings bank.

BRED Banque Populaire
   http://www.bred.fr/euro9798.htm

Caixa Galicia
   http://www.caixagalicia.es/MAPAWEB/mni1.htm

Caixa Geral de Depósitos
   http://www.cgd.pt/euro/Capa.htm

Caja de Ahorros de la Inmaculada
   http://www.cai.es/opc_3.html

Caja de Ahorros del Mediterráneo
   http://www.afi.es/saicam/CAM/EURO.HTM

Caja de Ahorros de Navarra
   http://www.accioneuro.can.es/

Caja de Ahorros de Ontynyent
   http://www.caixaontinyent.es/moneda.htm

Caja de Burgos
http://www.cajadeburgos.es/infoeuro.htm

Caja de Cataluña
http://cec.caixacatalunya.es/euro/pral_esp.html

Caja España
http://www.cajaespana.es/feuro.htm
    This is the Caja España's euro web page. It offers a very broad service on the
    impact of the euro in several areas (as well as on other EU-related issues of
    concern to the banking community and to its customers).

Caja Segovia
http://www.cajasegovia.es/EURO/Principa.htm

CARIPLO
http://redazione.cariplo.it/Consigli.nsf?OpenDatabase

Cassa di Risparmio di Udine e Pordenone
http://www.crup.it/prova.html

Cassa Rurale di Strembo, Bocenago e Caderzone
http://www.crsbc.it/indexeur.htm

CISF Bank
http://194.79.83.35/euro/cisf/

Cofinoga
http://www.cofinoga.fr/

Commerzbank
http://www.commerzbank.de/navigate/euro_frm.htm

Crediop
http://www.crediop.it/EURO/default.htm

Crédit Agricole du Nord
http:www.nordnet.fr/ca-nord/pages/ind_actu.htm

Crédit Commercial de France
http://www.ccf.fr/espace_euro/index.html

Crédit Industriel et Commercial
http://www.cic-banques.fr/grfs_dos.htm#NIVEAU-5

Crédit Local de France
http:www.clf.fr/PAGES/EURO/EURO.htm
    This is the main euro web page of the Crédit Local de France

Crédit Lyonnais
http://deef.creditlyonnais.fr/

Crédit Mutuel
http://www.cmutuel.com/home.html

Crédit Suisse
http://www.ska.com/economic-research/Euro/frmEuro.html

Crédit Suisse Asset Management
http://www.credis.de/Investmentperspektiven/euro.htm

Creditanstalt
http://www.creditanstalt.co.at/pid401D.shtml

Deutsche Bank
http://194.175.173.31/dbr/html_d/ewu.htm
    This is the euro web site of Deutsche Bank (in German and in English)
    entitled "Euro Aktuell."

Deutsche Bank España
http://www.deutsche-bank.es/naveg/euro_1.htm

DG Bank of Germany
http://www.dgbank.de/leistung/ag/eu/euu

Die-erste
http://www.erstebank.at/1nonjava/fshome.htm
    This site contains a euro calculator.

Dresdner Bank
http://www.dresdner-bank.de/f_firmen/u_europa/home.htm

Fortis
http://www.nl.fortis.com/euro/

Frankfurter Sparkasse 1822
http://www.fraspa1822.de/ewwu.html

Friesland Bank
http://www.friba.nl/html/euro.html

Générale de Banque
http://www.gbank.be/fr/business/euro/inleidi.htm

GZB Bank
http://www.gzb-bank.de/
    This is the web site of GZB-Bank of Germany. It offers links to two pages
    dedicated to the euro, entitled "euro" and "euro classic."

Hamburger Bank von 1861
http://www.hambank.de/euro/euro.htm

Hamburgische Landesbank Girozentrale
http://www.hamburglb.de/hlbwinfo/267e.htm

IKB Deutsche Industriebank AG
http://www.ikb.de/ger/eurotext.htm

ING
http://euro.ing.nl
    This is the eurodesk of the ING bank in Dutch and English.

Istituto Bancario San Paolo di Torino
  http://www.sanpaolo.it/euro/

JP Morgan
  http://www.jpmorgan.com/businesses/fx/emufactsheet/fs.html
    This is the euro web page of JP Morgan, which is entitled "EMU Fact Sheet."

Kredietbank
  http://www.kb.be/euro/alg/eurb01.htm
    This is the euro web site of Kredietbank (in Dutch, English, and French). It
    contains a wide range of documentation on the impact of the changeover on
    customers, with particular attention paid to corporate customers.

Kreissparkasse Gelnhausen
  http:ksk.gelnhausen.net/euro.htp

Kreissparkasse Hannover
  http://www.ksk-hannover.de/d16.html

Kreissparkasse Ludwigsburg
  http://www.ksklb.de/

La Caixa
  http://lacaixa.datalab.es/cast/infee_cs.html

Leonia Bank
  http://www.leonia.fi/emu/http://www.leonia.fi/emu/

LG-Bank
  http://www.lgbank.de/berechnungenf/euro.htm

Mediocredito Centrale
  http://www.mcc.it/euroindx.htm

Merita Bank
  http://www.merita.fi/EURO/

Naspa Bank
  http://www.naspa.de/1_1_1.htm

Openbank
  http://www.openbank.es/indicadores/homemastrich.htm

P.S.K. (Postbank—Austria)
  http://www.psk.co.at/EUROABC/index.html

Postbank (Germany)
  http://www.postbank.de/info/finanz.html

Postbank (Netherlands)
  http://www.postbank.nl/postbank/index.htm?ID=679&EID=13

Postipankki
  http://www.psp.fi/su/tanaan/1997/t10119

Quelle Bank
   http://www.quelle-bank.de/home/index.html

Rabobank
   http://www.rabobank.nl/euro/euro.htm

Raiffeisenbanken Gruppe
   http://www.raiffeisen.at/rbg/euinfo1.htm

Société Générale
   http://www.socgen.com/html/fr/act/euro/acue_f.htm

Société Générale Deutschland
   http://www.socgen.de/deutsch/Kunden/Eurocountdown/eurocount.htm

Sparkasse Aachen
   http://www.sparkasse-ac.de/

Sparkasse Essen
   http://www.sparkasse-essen.de/spkessen/spkessen.nsf/VwDocsToPublish
   /D010000LS?OpenDocument

Sparkassen im Internet
   http://www.snet.de/Information/index.html

Stadt Sparkasse Düsseldorf
   http://sskduesseldorf.de/ausland/euro.html

Steiermärkische Bank und Sparkassen
   http://www.bank-styria.co.at/

Svenska Handelsbanken
   http://www.handelsbanken.se/hemsidor.nsf/frameset/AktuelltEngFrameSet

Ulster Bank
   http://www.ulsterbank.com/ri/emu/emuintro.htm

Unibank
   http://www.unibank.dk/erhverv/oemu/oemu_frame.html

Unicaja
   http://correo.unicaja.es/eco/7_econo.htm

Vereinsbank
   http://www2.vereinsbank.de/?Category=/&Page=Vereinsbank

Volksbank Fürstenfeldbruck eG
   http://www.volksbank-ffb.de/waehrungsunion/waehrungsunion.htm

Westdeutsche Landesbank
   http://www.westlb.de/euro/

WGZ Bank
   http://www.wgz-bank.de/cgi-bin/softweb/ch2/p22.htm
      This is the euro web page of WGZ Bank of Germany, one of the common
      banking institutions of the cooperative banks of Germany. From this site

you may order four brochures in German on the impact of EMU on
corporate strategies in areas of the marketing, accounting, payment
systems, and law.

STOCK EXCHANGES, SECURITY SETTLEMENT SYSTEMS, PAYMENT SYSTEMS, AND SECURITY DEPOSITORIES

Deutsche Terminbörse
  http://www.exchange.de/specials/euroinfo.html

Euroclear
  http://www.euroclear.com

LIFFE
  http://www.liffe.com

MATIF
  http://www.matif.fr/matif/argueuro.htm

Sicovam
  http://www.sicovam.com/

Società per i servizi bancari
  http://www.ssb.net/euro/HTMLNS3/HOMEEURO.HTM

ASSOCIATIONS OF ENTERPRISES, COMMERCE, AND SERVICES

Associação Portuguesa das Empresas de Contabilidade
  http://www.centroatl.pt/ve679con.html

Association for the Monetary Union of Europe
  http://amue.lf.net/business/busiindx.htm

Cambres de Comerç, Indústria i Navegació de Catalunya
  http://www.cambrescat.es/economia/euro/euro002.htm

Camera di Commercio di Milano
  http://www.mi.camcom.it/euro/

Chambre de Commerce de Lille
  http://www.lille.cci.fr/dpi/euro04.html

Confesercenti
  http://www.confesercenti.it/eic.htm

Conseil National du Patronat Français
  http://www.cnpf.asso.fr/sommaire.htm#top

Dublin Chamber of Commerce
  http://www.dubchamber.ie/buscont/february97/euro.htm

Eurochambres
http://www.eurochambres.be/2news/ec2001k.htm

Eurocommerce
http://www.eurocommerce.be/epress97.htm#nov13
   This is the press release by Eurocommerce (the Brussels-based association of
   retail, wholesale, and international trade in the EU) outlining its position on
   the introduction of the euro.

Experts Comptables
http://www.euro-expert.com

Fédération des Experts Comptables Européens
http://www.euro.fee.be
   This is the euro information service of the Fédération des Experts Comptables
   Européens, the European Association of Accountants. It offers information
   in English, German, French, Italian, and (partially) Spanish. Check out its
   "Check-list on the introduction of the euro."

Foment del Treball Nacional
http://www.foment.com/binter.htm

Forfas
http://www.emuaware.forfas.ie/

Groupe Equinoxe
http://www.groupeequinoxe.com/site/ge/ge_tex/rapports/r_eu/r_emuan/r
_emuan_accu.html

Handelskammer Düsseldorf
http://www.forum.duesseldorf.ihk.de/zusatzseminare/euro.htm

Handwerkskammer Region Stuttgart
http://www.hwk-stuttgart.de/euro.htm

Indicod
http://www.indicod.it/euro/index.htm

Irish Business and Employers Confederation
http://www.ibec.ie/euro/
   This is the web site of the Euro Currency Countdown Campaign, managed by
   the Irish Business and Employers Confederation (IBEC) and supported by
   the European Commission.

Patronat Català Pro Europa
http://www.gencat.es/pcpe/euro.htm

Wirtschaftskammer Österreich
http://www.wk.or.at/ih_info/euro/euro.htm
   This is the euro-information platform of the Wirtschaftskammer Österreich,
   the Austrian Chamber of Commerce.

CONSULTANCY FIRMS IN THE BUSINESS AREA

Argandoña Asesores
> http://www.argandona-ases.es/aa/revista/euro.htm
>> This is the euro web page of the consultancy firm Argandoña Asesores of Barcelona. It contains information on the impact of the euro on corporations.

Askeaton
> http://www.askeaton.com/askeaton/euro.htm/
>> This is the home page of Askeaton, a consultancy firm that specializes in certain areas of international finance and that maintains contact with ISMA and ACI.

Cap Gemini
> http://www.capgemini.com/eng/issues/euro.html
>> This is the euro web page of the consultancy firm Cap Gemini. A list of euro contact persons is included in http://www.capgemini.com/way/emucom .htm.

Company Euro Associates
> http://www.euro-direct.com/default.html
>> This the web site of the Company Euro Associates. It provides general information on the euro and links to other web sites.

Coopers & Lybrand Germany
> http://www.colybrand.de/newsline/spiele/puzzle.html

Coopers & Lybrand UK
> http://www.uk.coopers.com/financialservices/bankersdigest/euro/euro.html

HAL
> http://www.halinfo.it/
>> This is the web site of HAL. It provides information concerning the euro project methodologies and products to address the changeover issue from a technical point of view.

KPMG
> http://www.kpmg.co.uk/uk/services/manage/emu.html
>> This is the KPMG web page on "Europe's Preparedness for EMU."

Mass maintenance
> http://www.massm.com/

Numéris
> http://www.capitaux.com/euro/
>> This is the euro web page of the French consultant Numéris. It contains material on the impact of the euro on corporations.

Orgaconseil/L'Argus
> http://www.orgaconseil.fr/mu_argus.htm

This web page contains an inquiry by the French consultancy firm
Orgaconseil/L'Argus, published in March 1997, on the impact of the single
currency on the insurance industry.

TCA Consulting
   http://www.tcaconsulting.co.uk/emu/index.htm
   This is the EMU web page of TCA Consulting. It provides articles and papers
   on euro issues.

TreasuryLog
   Target="_top">http://www.go-public.com/TreasuryLog/297/index.htm
   TreasuryLog is a project by a private consultancy firm in Austria called
   Schwabe, Ley and Greyner, which offers advice on euro cash management
   issues. A working group has been created and several surveys in reference to
   the project are available on this web page.

Varial®
   http:/www.varial.de/pages/euro-hot.htm
   This is the euro web page (in German) of a consultancy firm called Varial®,
   specializing in the impact of the euro on accounting. It contains a news
   service as well as a list of the key euro issues.

NEWSPAPERS, NEWSLETTERS, MAGAZINES, AND BIBLIOGRAPHIES

AGEFI
   http://www.agefi.fr/dossiers/eur/somm.htm
   This is the euro web page of the French weekly *AGEFI* (*Agence Financière*).
   It includes texts and links. Details of a conference on the euro can be found
   at the Internet address
      http://www.agefi.fr/seminaires/actes/euro.htm.

ANSA
   http://www.ansa.it/euro/index.htm
   This is a publication of news wires on the euro in Italian by the news agency
   ANSA. It summarises weekly initiatives on preparatory work in Italy.

Crédit Commercial de France
   http://www.ccf.fr/euro/informer/sel_euro.htm

EBN
   http://www.ebn.co.uk/Features/CountdownToEuro/
   This is the euro web page of EBN European Business Network. It offers the
   option of looking at some videos concerning the transition to the single
   currency.

Economist Intelligence Unit
   http://www.eiu.com/latest/rr_emu/emuintro.html

This is the euro web page of the Economist Intelligence Unit (EIU). It includes a report entitled "The pros and cons of EMU," by David Currie.

ecu-euro

http://www.ecu-activities.be

This is the web page of the magazine *ECU-euro* (published by Editions ecu activities a.s.b.l. and edited by Pierre Guimbretière), which is produced in English and French and specializes in issues concerning the transition to the single currency.

Euro-Impact

http://www.euro-impact.com

This is the web site of the monthly newsletter *Euro-Impact*. It provides extensive information on changeover issues.

Euro: moneda unica para Europa

http://www.geocities.com/WallStreet/8999/

This is a highly comprehensive and informative web page on the euro in Spanish.

Euromoney

http://www.euromoney.com/contents/publications/euroweek/ew.97/ew.97.530/ew.97.530.index.html

European Bond Commission of EFFAS

http://www.ukbc.org.uk/cgi-bin/ailsa/ukbc-emu/search?s_name

Expansión

http://www.recoletos.es/expansion/dossier/retos/pregunta.htm

Financial Times

http://www.ft.com/hippocampus/tpsemu.htm

Il Sole 24 Ore

http://www.ilsole24ore.it/euro/#top

This is the web site of the Italian economic daily newspaper *Il Sole 24 Ore* in Italian.

Institutions Européennes & Finance

http://ief.area-mundi.com

This is the web site of the *Institutions Européennes & Finance,* which is a highly informative monthly newsletter in French on preparations for EMU.

Tijd

http://www.tijd.be/tijdnet/forum/euro_bijlage/titels.htm

This is the euro web page of the Belgian economic daily newspaper *Tijd*. It contains specific information on the preparations for the euro in Belgium and explains the impact of the euro on citizens, corporations, and investors.

GLOSSARY

Bretton Woods   Landmark international agreement signed by representatives of 44 nations in Bretton Woods, New Hampshire, in 1944. It featured a system of fixed exchange rates that was designed to usher in an era of economic stability in the postwar period. The Bretton Woods exchange rate agreements fell apart in the early 1970s.

common market   Any geographic area characterized by the free movement of goods, services, labor, and capital. In Europe, the term has been used to describe the EEC, the EC, and the first stage of EMU alternatively. The creation of the European common market was technically completed by the end of 1992.

convergence criteria   Five economic requirements regarding price stability, government financial profiles, exchange rates, and long-term interest rates that EU countries must fulfill in order to qualify for monetary union.

ECOFIN   Name given to European Council meetings when they are composed of economics and finance ministers from the 15 EU member states.

Economic and Monetary Union (EMU)   A specific international cooperation agreement defined in the Treaty on European Union that involves the strengthening of the common market and the introduction of a single currency in three stages.

euro   Official name of the single currency introduced in Euroland on January 1, 1999. Before December 1995, known as the "ecu."

Euroland   Term used to refer to the 11 EU nations that introduced the euro as legal tender on January 1, 1999.

European Central Bank (ECB)   Monetary authority and central bank of the single-currency zone, responsible for the formulation and implementation of monetary policy in Euroland. The ECB is located in Frankfurt, Germany.

European Commission   The executive and administrative institution of the European Union responsible for implementing EU legislation.

European Community (EC)   Refers to the 1967 merger of the European Economic Community (EEC) with two other major European treaties in existence at that time: the European Coal and Steel Community (ECSC) and the European Atomic Energy Community (Euratom). The EC became part of the EU in 1993.

European Council Critically important council composed of representatives from the governments of the 15 member states of the European Union, though committee composition changes depending on the issues being discussed. Council often consists, for example, of the 15 heads of state of the EU.

European Currency Unit (Ecu) A theoretical basket of currencies composed of fixed amounts of 12 out of the 15 currencies of the European Union. The Ecu does not exist in note and coin form but has been used as a unit of account and trade since the late 1970s.

European Economic Community (EEC) An outdated term that refers to the international cooperation agreement created by the Treaty of Rome, a treaty signed by the governments of France, West Germany, Belgium, the Netherlands, Luxembourg, and Italy. The EEC became part of the EC in 1967.

European Monetary Institute (EMI) Predecessor of the European Central Bank (ECB), this institution was founded in 1994 to prepare the general and operational framework for the conduct of monetary policy in Euroland. The EMI became the ECB on June 1, 1998.

European Monetary System (EMS) A monetary cooperation agreement created in 1979 for the purpose of stabilizing exchange rate fluctuations between EEC member countries. The EMS featured an exchange rate mechanism (ERM), based on central rates around which any two currencies were allowed to fluctuate without central bank intervention. With the advent of EMU, the original ERM has now given way to ERM II, designed to stabilize exchange rates between the euro and the currencies of other EU countries.

European System of Central Banks (ESCB) Name given to the central banking system of Euroland as a whole, a system that consists of the ECB and 11 national central banks.

European Union (EU) Name of the international cooperation agreement created by the Treaty on European Union, which currently consists of 15 nations. The European Union features three general areas of cooperation: (1) economic and monetary union, (2) foreign and security policy, and (3) justice, law, and domestic affairs.

euro zone Alternative name for Euroland.

Gross Domestic Product (GDP) The total market value of all goods and services produced in a given area in a specific period of time (usually one year).

Maastricht criteria   Alternative name for the convergence criteria.

Maastricht Treaty   Alternative name for the Treaty on European Union.

monetary policy   Policies developed by central banks with the intention of influencing and stabilizing inflation. Generally conducted by manipulating a region's interest and exchange rates.

money supply   The total stock of money in an economy, usually denoted by the specific terms M1, M2, or M3. M3, for instance, is a statistical measure that includes cash-in-hand as well as checking account balances and short-term deposits.

repurchase agreement (repo)   A transaction involving the sale of an asset to another party with the explicit promise to repurchase the asset at a later date for a different price. Repos function like loans and are used as credit instruments by the ECB to control liquidity to the banking system.

Stability & Growth Pact   Name given to several agreements guiding fiscal and economic policies of countries adopting the euro. Its most important feature is an excessive-deficit procedure, which imposes substantial fines on countries unable to keep their annual public deficits under predetermined levels.

TARGET   Trans-European Automated Real-time Gross settlement Express Transfer system that links national payment settlement systems and operates in euros. Indispensible for the effective and efficient transfer of payments from one party to another in Euroland.

Treaty on European Union   Treaty founding the European Union, signed on February 7, 1992, and effective on November 1, 1993. It amended the 1958 Treaty of Rome establishing the EEC and broadened western European international cooperation well beyond the economic arena.

REFERENCES

1. Anonymous, "Die Bürger fühlen sich besser beraten," *Handelsblatt,* June 19, 1998.

2. Courtis, N., "Euro banknotes: how not to introduce a new currency," *Central Banking,* vol. 8, no. 3, winter (December/February) 1997/1998, pp. 63–64.

3. Gotta, F., "Produktion des Euro kostet Milliarden," *Die Welt,* March 25, 1998.

4. Willman, J., "Euro design may confuse EU vending machines," *Financial Times,* February 13, 1998.

5. Berschens, R., and Dunkel, M., "Weltmacht Europa," *Wirtschaftswoche,* no. 19, April 30, 1998, pp. 28–40.

6. Duisenberg, W., "EMU, magnet or bone of contention?" *De Nederlandsche Bank Quarterly Bulletin,* June 1996, p. 1.

7. Churchill, Winston, Zürich speech, September 19, 1946, cited in W. Lipgens and W. Loth (eds.), *Documents in the History of European Integration,* vol. 3, Berlin: Walter de Gruyter, 1988, pp. 662–66.

8. Duisenberg, W. F., "Why EMU?" *De Nederlandshe Bank Quarterly Bulletin,* June 1996, pp. 15–16.

9. Kohl, H., "EWWU Eckstein für Europa," *Bank Information und Genossenschafts Forum,* Jan. 1997, pp. 4–5.

10. Association for the Monetary Union of Europe, "Euro preparation guide for companies," Paris, June 1997.

11. Cohen, A., "The Euro May Be Good for You," *Financial Times,* November 20, 1997.

12. Emerson, M., Gros D., Italianer, A., Pisani-Ferry, J., and Reichenbach, H., *One Market, One Money,* Oxford University Press, 1992, p. 63.

13. Riess, S., "Euro: 100 Fakten, die Ihr Geld retten," Munich: Wilhelm Heyne Verlag, 1997, p. 80.

14. Coman, J., "Land of Hope and Glory?" *The European,* April 27–May 5, 1998.

15. Bergsten, C. F., "The Dollar Will Have to Make Room for the Euro," *International Herald Tribune,* December 17, 1997.

16. Taylor, C., "The Economics and Politics of EMU," in *EMU Explained: Markets and Monetary Union,* edited by Pitchford, R. and Cox, A., Reuters, 1997, p. 23.

17. Deputy Secretary of the Treasury Lawrence H. Summers, "EMU: An American View of Europe," *Euromoney Conference,* New York City, April 30, 1997.

18. Bank of International Settlements, *Central Bank Survey of Foreign Exchange and Derivatives Market Activity,* Basle, 1995.

19. Portes, R., and Rey, H., "The emergence of the euro as an international currency," in *EMU: Prospects and Challenges for the Euro,* edited by D. Begg, J. Hagan, C. Wyplosz, and K. Zimmerman, Oxford: Blackwell, 1998, pp. 307–332.

20. Duisenberg, W., "Enorme Vorteile," Interview in *Manager Magazin,* June 26, 1997, p. 167.

21. Maddison, A., "Monitoring the World Economy, 1820–1992," OECD Development Centre Study, Paris: OECD, 1995, p. 255.

22. Anonymous, "Automatenwirtschaft: Euro kommt zu früh," *Der Tagesspiegel,* January 15, 1998.

23. Münchau, W., "Big Companies May Face $50bn Emu Cost," *Financial Times,* December 8, 1997.

24. Duisenberg, W., "Enorme Vorteile," Interview in *Manager Magazin,* June 26, 1997, p. 167.

25. Buckman, R. and Kim, J., "Euro's Advent Means Major Headaches for Financial Firms," *The Wall Street Journal Europe,* March 11, 1998.

26. Cohen, A., "The Euro May Be Good For You," *Financial Times,* November 20, 1997, p. 11.

27. Friedman, M., "Why Europe Can't Afford the Euro," *The Times,* November 19, 1997.

28. Anonymous, "Is the Single Market Working?" *The Economist,* February 17, 1996, p. 30.

29. Feldmann, H., "Economic and Political Risks of Economic and Monetary Union," *Intereconomics,* vol. 32, no. 3, May–June 1997, p. 114.

30. Santer, J., "The advantages of EMU," *Economic & Financial Review,* vol. 2, no. 2, summer 1995, p. 48.

31. Currie, D., "The Pros and Cons of EMU," Special Report by HM Treasury, July 1997, p. 8.

32. Dahrendorf, R., "Disunited by a common currency," *New Statesman,* February 20, 1998, pp. 32–33.

33. Sutherland, P. "The Case for EMU," *Foreign Affairs,* vol. 76, no. 1, January/February 1997, p. 10.

34. George, E., quoted in Chote, R., "UK bank governor casts doubt on single currency," *Financial Times,* September 23, 1997.

35. Kissinger, H., "A New Union in Europe," *Washington Post,* May 12, 1998.

36. Feldmann, H., "Economic and political risks of European Monetary Union," *Intereconomics,* vol. 32, no. 3, May/June 1997, pp. 107–115.

37. McCauley, R. N., "The euro and the dollar," *Central Banking,* vol. 8, no. 4, spring (March/May) 1998, pp. 62–64.

38. Tietmeyer, H., "European monetary integration and its implications for the international monetary system," Lecture in honor of Professor Xenophon Zolotas, October 17, 1997.

39. Begg, D., Giavazzi, F. and Wyplosz, C., "Options for the Future Exchange Rate Policy of the EMU," Center for Economic Policy Research, Occasional Paper No. 17, cited in Münchau, W., "Euro exchange rate policy is still the big uncertainty," *Financial Times,* January 6, 1998.

40. Bank of International Settlements, *Central Bank Survey of Foreign Exchange and Derivatives Market Activity,* Basle, 1995.

41. ECU Institute, *International Currency Competition and the Future Role of the Single European Currency,* Kluwer Law International, Dordrecht.

42. Shirref, D., "European Monetary Union: The outside view. What will be the effect of European economic and monetary union (EMU) on the rest of the world?" *Euromoney,* December 1996, pp. 113–116.

43. Laughland, J., "Why a single rate hurts all," *The European,* March 23–29, 1998.

44. Duisenberg, W., "From the EMI to the ESCB: Achievements and Challenges," Speech delivered to the Luxembourg Bankers' Association and the International Bankers Club, September 12, 1997, p. 3.

45. Marsden, K., "Europe's Best Defense?" *The Wall Street Journal Europe,* June 8, 1998.

46. Roach, S., "Europe's dilemmas revisited," *Financial Times,* May 27, 1998.

47. Kaletsky, A., "The euro: how they got away with it," *The Times,* March 3, 1998.

48. Sigurdsson, J. "Monetary Union and European Securities Markets Implications for Multilateral Issuers," *Economic and Financial Review,* vol. 5, no. 1, spring (January/March) 1998, pp. 17–33.

49. Freedman, J., "Banks Outside the EMU Still Must Adapt Euro," *The Wall Street Journal Europe,* August 27, 1997.

50. Hamilton, A., "Euro-markets face big bang. Only the fittest banks will survive the revolution," *The European,* June 26–July 2, 1997.

51. Adams, R., "EURO: Vulnerable industries identified," *Financial Times,* August 10, 1998.

52. Anonymous, "European banks, Survival tactics. Should European banks fear or welcome a single currency? The experience of Belgium offers a guide," *The Economist,* August 9, 1997, pp. 69–70.

53. Anonymous, "Euro brings war of the indices," *Financial Times,* February 3, 1998.

INDEX

ABOUT THE AUTHOR

Christian Chabot worked in the Economics and EMU divisions of the Deutsche Bundesbank, where he dealt firsthand with the theoretical and technical aspects of monetary union. Sponsored by a 1997–1998 Robert Bosch Foundation Fellowship, Mr. Chabot had an intimate look at the euro's preparatory stages. Prior to his work in Europe, Mr. Chabot was employed as a Senior Economic Analyst for Cornerstone Research. He is a graduate of Stanford University (B.S.), where he received the Firestone Medal for Excellence in Research, and England's University of Sussex (M.Sc.), which awarded him the Rothwell Prize for Outstanding Research. Mr. Chabot is currently based in Palo Alto, California.